A Son is Promised

A SON IS PROMISED

Christ in the Psalms

Harry Uprichard

 EVANGELICAL PRESS

EVANGELICAL PRESS
12 Wooler Street, Darlington, Co. Durham, DL1 1RQ, England

British Library Cataloguing in Publication Data available

ISBN 0 85234 327 2

Printed and bound in Great Britain at the Bath Press, Avon.

Contents

Acknowledgements

Sincere thanks are expressed to all who have helped with this book: to Mrs Daniel McKee for willingly giving of her time, patience and care in typing the manuscript; to my friend and colleague Rev. N. W. McAuley, for suggestions, advice and proof-reading; to the staff of Evangelical Press for their interest in, and supervision of, this venture; and to my wife Maisie, for all her love and encouragement in writing.

Harry Uprichard
Trinity Manse, Ahoghill,
November 1994

Introduction

'Read me a psalm,' people sometimes say. So I read Psalm 23 to remind them of God's shepherding love, or Psalm 40 to recall their experience of saving faith, or Psalm 27 to assure them that God hides them in his secret tent in time of trouble, or part of Psalm 119 to revive their hope in God's Word. 'I love the Psalms,' they often say. All Christians do. The Psalms are so warm and personal, so alive with the reality of God, so relevant to every changing circumstance of life. We can read, sing or repeat them. The effect is the same. We know what Luther meant when he described the Psalms as 'the Bible in miniature'.

There is even more to the Psalms than that, however. Allowing the above, we have only scratched the surface, skirted around the shallows. We need to launch out into the deep. Jesus points the way: 'This is what I told you while I was still with you: Everything must be fulfilled that is written about me in the Law of Moses, the Prophets and the Psalms' (Luke 24:44). As Jesus opened their minds to understand the Scriptures the sequence was almost incredible. What was written was that Christ would suffer, rise from the dead on the third day and that repentance and forgiveness of sins would be preached in his name, beginning at Jerusalem. Everything about Jesus was in these three sections of the Old Testament — the Law, the Prophets and the Writings, which began with the Psalms — and it was there, down to the finest detail, for our instruction.

Of course, Jesus had done precisely the same thing earlier, not to the whole group of disciples, but to the two dispirited followers on the Emmaus road. Then he began with the earlier two sections, the Law and the Prophets, but obviously went on to include the Psalms within the Writings, in his exposition: 'And beginning with Moses and all the Prophets, he explained to them what was said in all the Scriptures concerning himself' (Luke 24:27).

The result in both instances was stupendous. The two, who were no longer downhearted, for their hearts burned within them as Jesus opened the Scriptures to them, trudged the eleven kilometres back to Jerusalem that very evening to tell the others that they had met the risen Lord. The disciples eventually made their way to the vicinity of Bethany, saw Jesus taken up to heaven and then returned to Jerusalem, not to get over the hallucination and pick up the threads of a purposeless and lonely life, but to remain with great joy and continuing praise in the Jerusalem temple. The Christ of Old Testament Scripture, fulfilled in Jesus of Nazareth, had transformed their lives. They were living witnesses to that. Even though he was gone to heaven, he was still, in a sense, with them, burning in their hearts through the Law of Moses, the Prophets and the Psalms.

Most Christians dabble in the Old Testament, a verse here, a verse there, a promise to lean on, a warning to take seriously, a character to follow because of success, a lifestyle to avoid because of failure. But large tracts of territory remain undiscovered, like jungle needing to be cleared or new seas needing to be mapped. Above all, there is no continuity, no coherent thread, no consistent story-line. The bottom line is that there is no need to find one, for the general impression is that the Old Testament is preparatory anyway, superseded by the New, the shadow replaced by the substance, the law abolished in favour of grace. Why bother with the Old Testament at all?

The result of this way of thinking is a distortion. The Old becomes a disposable introduction, the New a second volume without a first. The Bible is divided, its unity destroyed. Discontinuity, not progression, marks the pattern of revelation. Yet Jesus' view contradicts all this. He quotes the Old Testament as the Word of God, uses its teaching to fire the early church and, above all, gives us a key to understanding it. It is all about himself: Christ is what the Old Testament is about — the Law, the Prophets and the Writings, down to the minutest detail, not just primarily, but totally and exclusively. Christ is written large on every page and in every verse. He is the story-line of all Scripture, both Old and New Testaments alike.

Our study of 'Christ in the Psalms' takes its inspiration from this. A word about methodology at this point: how are we to interpret the Old Testament like this? What guidelines are we to follow? What parameters will restrain fancy from running riot in our minds and prevent all sorts of hare-brained interpretations from emerging?

We shall select some psalms which have clearly a Messianic content, that is, which point forward prophetically to Christ. We shall confirm that choice in our minds by discovering quotations from these psalms in the New Testament. More than that, gauging the Messianic tenor of these psalms through the quotations in the New Testament, we shall first establish the broad lines of that teaching in the psalm itself and then move forwards to the fulfilment in the New Testament, using the New Testament quotations as a guideline. This will preserve both continuity and progression. We will interpret Scripture by Scripture. It will guard against fanciful misrepresentation and lead us in the right direction.

The emerging pattern becomes exciting. Christ is the anointed king of Psalm 2, the second Adam of Psalm 8, the righteous sufferer of Psalm 69, the dying victim of Psalm 22, the perfect sacrifice of Psalm 40, the high priest of Psalm 110 and the spiritual temple of Psalm 118.

The list is selective, not exhaustive. Other psalms will yield similar exciting finds. The process is unlimited. Indeed, if everything written in the Law, the Prophets and the Writings about Christ is fulfilled in Christ, then there is further work to be done, with equally heart-warming results, throughout the entire Old Testament. I have attempted this, to a limited degree already, in *A Son is Given,* examining some selected passages from Isaiah. The process is a 'starter', a mere introduction to the very heartbeat of Old Testament Scripture. It begs further investigation until the whole of the Old is ablaze with the truth of the New. 'The New is in the Old concealed; the Old is in the New revealed,' said Augustine. Let us use this method, Scripture interpreting Scripture, to discover hidden in the Old Testament further pearls of great price about Christ, our Lord and Saviour.

If this sparks off a fresh understanding of Scripture, if it helps us view the Old Testament in a better way and see the New in a clearer light, if our hearts begin to burn within us so that we worship, return with joy and stay continually with the Christ of the Psalms till he comes from heaven to take us home, any effort in writing will be more than amply rewarded.

'Were not our hearts burning within us while he talked with us on the road and opened the Scriptures to us?' (Luke 24:32).

'When he had led them out to the vicinity of Bethany, he lifted up his hands and blessed them. While he was blessing them, he left them and was taken up into heaven. Then they worshipped him and returned to Jerusalem with great joy. And they stayed continually at the temple, praising God' (Luke 24:50-53).

Deo gloria sola.

1.
Anointed King

Psalm 2 is a royal psalm. It celebrates the greatness of the King of Israel. The historical background may well be the occasion when David became king in Jerusalem (2 Sam. 5). David had come a long and perilous way to the throne, but finally he was acclaimed king and the height of his power was attributed to the fact that God was with him. Because of this, he became more and more powerful.

The psalm is full of the majesty and sovereignty of Israel's king. It recounts this in a number of ways, stressing, above all, the position of the king as a personal office appointed by God. Indeed, the terms are such that it appears to go beyond the limits of human kingship and suggests divine prerogative. Even among the Jews the second psalm was regarded as Messianic, that is, pointing forward as a prophecy to the coming Messiah. A twelfth-century Jewish scholar, Jarchi, maintained, 'Our doctors have expounded this Psalm of the Messiah; but we may answer to heretics [Christians] it is expedient to interpret it of David's person, as the words sound.' However, the terms used to describe the king, the fact that they are unlikely in their fullest expression to depict only David and his heirs, and the way in which the New Testament writers interpret the psalm all suggest that Psalm 2 is Messianic. It is a prophecy of the coming Christ.

Anointed

The psalm begins with a startling question:

'Why do the nations conspire
and the peoples plot in vain?

> The kings of the earth take their stand
> > and the rulers gather together against the Lord
> > and against his Anointed One.
> "Let us break their chains," they say,
> > "and throw off their fetters"'

(Ps. 2:1-3).

It is incredible that nations and peoples so conspire. Their efforts will prove futile. God will laugh and scoff at them from heaven. He will rebuke them and strike terror into their hearts. The reason for this divine reaction is clear. The surrounding nations have dared to attack God's anointed king. They have plotted against the man chosen and appointed by God. They will not do that and escape the consequences.

Anointing was very important in the Old Testament. It involved pouring oil over a person's head to denote God's choice for a particular task. The oil represented the Spirit of God and meant divine appointment. It was a sacred act that required absolute obedience, for God's choice and authority lay behind the appointment. Priests, kings and even, on occasion, prophets were anointed. All three offices are eventually combined in Jesus Christ.

'Anointed One' in Hebrew is translated by 'Messiah' in English. 'Christ' in Greek has precisely the same meaning. The Messiah of the Old Testament points forward to the Christ of the New Testament. However dimly the Jews understood the term, they gradually became aware that it went far beyond David, to David's greater Son. This was one reason why they accepted the second psalm as Messianic. The rage and fury of the nations against David was understandable historically. It was a common occurrence in his day. Such plotting against David, God's 'Anointed One', would prove futile. But the futility of opposition becomes really clear when David's greater Son is considered. It is not only futile; it is arrogant and sinful. Opposition to God's Messiah is doomed to failure.

Enthroned

The king of the second psalm is not only anointed, but also enthroned by God. There are not only appointment but coronation rites involved in his royal position. The terms are worth noting:

> "'I have installed my king
>   on Zion, my holy hill."
> I will proclaim the decree of the Lord:
> He said to me, "You are my Son;
>   today I have become your Father'"
>
> (Ps. 2:6-7).

The king is appointed by divine decree. It is a decree proclaiming the king as Son of God. The office is rooted in a relationship with God. In the ancient world, kings were often regarded as sons of the gods, but this was in a mystical or magical sense. It gave an aura of mystery and authority to their rule. Here the situation is quite different. The relationship springs neither from mystery nor magic but from covenant. It is part of the relationship which God maintains with his people in the covenant he made with them.

God had specifically promised this to David and his line: 'I will establish the throne of his kingdom for ever. I will be his father, and he shall be my son' (2 Sam. 7:13-14). Relationship was of the very essence of God's covenant with his people. When God had approached Abraham, it was with a view to being a God to him and to his family after him. When God renewed his covenant with Moses, for the clan had now become a nation, it was again couched in terms of intimate relationship. Israel would be a holy nation, a kingdom of priests, God's own prized possession. Belonging lay at the heart of the covenant: 'I will be their God, they will be my people.' Now in 2 Samuel 7:5-16, as God encourages David through his solemn covenant promise, the covenant points forward to the future and the terms of relationship become more personal and intense. The Davidic dynasty represents Israel and is related to God on a father/son basis. The king is God's son. Israel are God's people. God is the eternal Father.

The fact that God would establish 'the throne of his kingdom for ever' (2 Sam. 7:13) throws the entire promise into a context far beyond that of David's dynasty. It points forward to the Messiah whose rule would be everlasting. Similarly, the father/son relationship in Psalm 2 goes beyond David's success in Jerusalem, or the future fortunes of his house. It anticipates the rule of Christ, the Messiah. It has a future and eternal dimension.

Empowered

The king is anointed, enthroned and empowered for office:

> 'Ask of me,
>   and I will make the nations your inheritance,
>   the ends of the earth your possession.
> You will rule them with an iron sceptre;
>   you will dash them to pieces like pottery'
>
> (Ps. 2:8-9).

The power of the king is vividly portrayed. There is a construc-
tive aspect of rule of government with an iron rod or sceptre. Behind
this is the image of the shepherd, who uses his staff not only to beat
off marauders, but to sort out the flock (Lev. 27:32; Ezek. 20:37; cf.
Ps. 23:4). Isaiah depicts God's Servant, the Branch from Jesse, as
striking the earth with the rod of his mouth and slaying the wicked
with the breath of his lips (Isa. 11:4). There is also a destructive
aspect of defeat and retribution. This is described as the king dashing
his enemies to pieces like pottery. It recalls Jeremiah in the Valley
of Ben Hinnom when, at God's command, he shatters the clay jar
before the people and proclaims God's word of judgement to them.
The king's power is absolute, whether used in governing his people
or destroying his enemies.

Again, the language of Psalm 2 goes beyond the house of Judah.
These very same attributes of rule and judgement are referred by the
prophets to the coming Messiah. Absolute rule is promised, not only
over the surrounding nations, but to 'the ends of the earth' (Ps. 2:8).
Absolute rule demands abject obedience, and that to 'the Son'.
Kings of the earth are summoned to wisdom, to be reconciled to
God's Son, whose wrath can instantly flare up in destruction (Ps.
2:10-12). The terms may recall David but clearly they have a wider
reference. The psalm is not simply a coronation anthem but a
prophecy of the power of the future Messiah. It cannot be contained
in David's dynasty. It looks forward to great David's greater Son,
anointed, enthroned and empowered, as King of kings and Lord of
lords.

Jesus: the anointed King

As a boy, I vaguely remember the coronation of Queen Elizabeth II. After the event we were escorted as a school to the local cinema where we saw a film of the proceedings. Watching a rerun of this recently on television brought the grandeur of it all home to me again, the sense of sadness and yet hope in the royal decree proclaimed to the present queen as she stepped from the royal aircraft to learn officially of her father's death: 'The king is dead, long live the queen.' The symbolism of the anointing behind the curtained enclosure during the coronation ceremony, the chanting by the choir of those words from Scripture in the aria 'Zadok the priest, Nathan the prophet, long live the king,' the raised arms of the archbishop as he placed the crown on the queen's head, the united voices of the peers dressed in their robes standing and acclaiming their sovereign, the sight of the queen on her throne, a sceptre in one hand and an orb in the other — it was all there, all these elements of dignity and splendour so prominent in the second psalm: a monarch anointed, enthroned, empowered for office. To me it was like a preview of a greater monarch on a greater throne, full of the majesty and glory of God's sovereignty. This is the scenario of the second psalm. It is truly Messianic.

The New Testament quotes the second psalm on a number of occasions. Christ comes into prominence in these New Testament references. They provide insights into Christ's kingly glory which otherwise would be missed. They teach valuable lessons about the Christian's daily experience of Christ as King. They focus on perspectives of Christ's kingship from the Psalms which are not as clearly evident in the Law and Prophets of the Old Testament. They give a challenging overview of Christ's kingship prophetically announced and dynamically fulfilled in the sovereignty of Jesus of Nazareth.

His lordship

The anointing of the psalmist's king is fulfilled in the lordship of Christ. In one remarkable instance where the psalm is plainly quoted, it is lordship over the nations in a time of desperate need

(Acts 4:23-31). This is fulfilled in the prayer life of the early church. Peter and John had healed a lame man at the temple gate. As a result of this and their subsequent preaching, they were summoned to appear before the Jewish court of the Sanhedrin. The Jews found themselves powerless to prevent future Christian outreach and, after threatening the apostles, released them. When Peter and John returned to the believers in Jerusalem, the church prayed to God about the situation. It was a remarkable prayer. Of the 134 words comprising it, twenty-seven are quoted from the second psalm. The portion quoted focuses on the anointing of the psalmist's Messiah and the futility of opposing him:

'Why do the nations rage
    and the peoples plot in vain?
The kings of the earth take their stand
    and the rulers gather together
against the Lord
    and against his Anointed One'
                                    (Acts 4:25-26; cf. Ps. 2:1-2).

His lordship rooted in the Trinity

The believers' perception of Jesus through this psalm is astounding. How do they see Jesus? Who is he? What is the nature of his work? All of these important questions are answered by the Christians as they meditate on the second psalm in prayer. Jesus is the Anointed One, the Messiah, the Christ. After quoting the psalm, the believers twice in their prayer refer to Jesus as God's anointed servant: 'your holy servant Jesus whom you anointed' (Acts 4:27), 'the name of your holy servant Jesus' (Acts 4:30). Apart from the specific reference to anointing, the whole drift of their petition in fact identifies Jesus quite clearly with the 'Anointed One' of Psalm 2.

The context of the prayer in which this identification occurs makes the perception even more impressive. Jesus is not only Messiah; he is divine, the Son within the triune Godhead. These Christians invoke God the Father, sovereign in creation and providence: 'Sovereign Lord, ... you made the heaven and the earth and the sea, and everything in them' (Acts 4:24); 'They did what your power and will had decided beforehand should happen' (Acts 4:28).

They recognize God the Spirit, sovereign in revelation: 'You spoke by the Holy Spirit through the mouth of your servant, our father David' (Acts 4:25). In acclaiming Jesus as God's anointed servant through whose name, not only had the cripple been healed, but miraculous signs and wonders could be done, they are virtually ascribing deity to Jesus. Jesus, through whose authority alone salvation comes, is on a par with God the Father and God the Spirit. God the Father creates and provides, God the Spirit reveals and God the Son redeems. This is the force of their calling Jesus God's 'servant' (Acts 4:25-27). Calvin writes, 'Thy holy Son Jesus. The Grecians use the very same word which I translated even now, servant, when mention was made of David, for they call *paida* sometimes a servant, sometimes a son; and David is so called because he was the minister of God, as well as ruling the people as in the office of a prophet; but this word, son, agreeth better with the person of Christ...'

Jesus of Nazareth is not just God's 'Anointed One' of Psalm 2:1-2; he is God's 'Son' of Psalm 2:7. Jesus is both Christ and Son of God. In this way he is God's promised King. Jesus' lordship over the nations is rooted in his messiahhood and sonship. Fearful believers at Jerusalem, as they addressed God in prayer, were clearly aware of that. Their point of reference for it was the second psalm.

His lordship revealed in Scripture

The believers' identification of their enemies was simple and direct. They specify the opposition in terms of the king's enemies in Psalm 2. The allusions are defined: 'Indeed Herod and Pontius Pilate met together with the Gentiles and the people of Israel in this city to conspire against your holy servant Jesus, whom you anointed' (Acts 4:27).

In today's terms, we might regard their use of Scripture as speculative. We might think that the pressed circumstances which they faced were making them 'read out' of Scripture what was not in it. But their view is delightfully simple and disarming. If Jesus of Nazareth is the anointed king of the second psalm, then 'the nations' and 'the peoples', 'the kings of the earth' and 'the rulers' must have their counterparts today. It was not fanciful speculation, but faith in Scripture which made the second psalm real to them in prayer. The lordship of Christ over the nations became relevant to their desperate need because they applied Scripture directly to their situation. The lordship of Christ was not theoretical but locked into the realities around them. These realities were the battlefield where Christ's triumphant lordship would be displayed. They interpret Scripture in the light of the lordship of Christ. This stimulates their praying.

The believers' vision in prayer was inspiring. This also came from the psalm: '"Now, Lord, consider their threats and enable your servants to speak your word with great boldness. Stretch out your hand to heal and perform miraculous signs and wonders through the name of your holy servant Jesus." After they prayed, the place where they were meeting was shaken. And they were all filled with the Holy Spirit and spoke the word of God boldly' (Acts 4:29-31).

The sovereignty of his lordship

The results of their praying were exciting beyond measure. The Christians translated their experience of Jesus' lordship in the past into prayer to help them in the present and to give them hope for the future. The power of Jesus' lordship is sovereign because it is eternal. As God's anointed King, he is the same yesterday, today and for ever. Jesus is great David's greater Son. They, no doubt, had in mind the healing of the cripple at the temple and, beyond that, the miraculous signs and wonders from the Day of Pentecost until the present. But before them loomed the threats of their enemies. They absorbed these threats in prayer as they identified them with the futile raging of the psalmist's foes. By faith they envisaged Christ's lordship in future miracles accomplished in his name as God's anointed Son. Whatever the 'bad news' of their enemies' threats, the 'good news' of Jesus' lordship outweighed it. Their faith in prayer received impetus as they directly meditated on the psalm and applied it literally to their circumstances. Without the anointed King of the second psalm they would have been prayerless and hopeless.

The answer to their prayer came in a remarkable way. The 'shaking' of the place where they met was certainly extraordinary (Acts 4:31), but there were no miraculous healings immediately. These came, as Luke records, later in the story after the treachery of Ananias and Sapphira (Acts 5:12-16). The immediate sequel of that prayer meeting was a filling of the Holy Spirit and a boldness in preaching God's Word. This latter term was used for liberty of speech and describes a freedom and forthrightness of proclamation not previously experienced. Luke goes on to mention a fresh dimension of unity, fellowship and practical caring among the believers (Acts 4:32-37). The immediate results of prayer were more evident within the church than outside it: a new dimension of the Spirit, of the Word and of fellowship. The lordship of Christ over the nations in this time of desperate need was first of all inspiring the church in order eventually to dominate the world. Revival of the church preceded evangelization of the lost. This came about when believers took the anointed king of the second psalm seriously.

I had been working in my present sphere of ministry for quite a number of years, praying earnestly, expounding the Word as clearly as possible, pastoring the flock with concern. We had seen some come to faith in Christ but longed for yet more. I was conscious of God's sovereignty in the work and the need for continuing prayer. Increasingly the burden for prayer weighed heavy on our hearts. Jesus' words about the healing of the demonic boy were constantly in mind: 'This kind can come out only by prayer' (Mark 9:29).

We concentrated more urgently on prayer individually and corporately. Remarkable things began to happen. People became concerned about spiritual realities. One occasion in particular lingers in my mind. I had finished a talk to some students and had time to spare before the mid-week meeting. I remember asking God specifically for blessing on his Word that evening. To my surprise — though I ought not to have been surprised — a young woman came to faith in Christ that night. In the desperate circumstances of spiritual barrenness we prayed for the power of Jesus the anointed King. We recognized the enemy as a dead, evangelical orthodoxy bereft of spiritual power. The vision which inspired our praying was that of Jesus, the anointed Son of God. We reaped the results of Christ's lordship through prayer to Jesus our King. Without this, we were hopeless and our efforts futile. With it, we realized things beyond human expectations. We began to share, in some small way, in what the Jerusalem church experienced through the Christ of the second psalm. Revival of the church in prayer was preceding evangelization of the lost. The lordship of the anointed Christ — triune in person, revealed in Scripture and sovereign in demonstration — was making itself known through the prayers of God's people by the power of the Holy Spirit.

His sonship

The enthronement of the psalmist's king is fulfilled in the sonship of Christ. The words in the psalm at the very centre of this enthronement declare the sonship of the king who is installed in Jerusalem:

> 'He said to me, "You are my Son,
>   today I have become your Father"'
>
>   (Ps. 2:7).

These words are alluded to and quoted in the New Testament to stress Christ's sonship. In this case, by way of contrast to the anointing, the references to enthronement in the psalm occur not just once, but in various parts of the New Testament. This variety makes even more impressive the fulfilment of the psalmist's enthronement in Christ's sonship. Repeated mention of Psalm 2:7 is like the recurring theme in a symphony. The different settings provide the variations. The central message comes through more forcefully because of this presentation.

His baptism

The baptism of Jesus marks the anointing of Christ's sonship. It was an impressive scene. Among the striking features on that occasion was the voice from heaven uttering the words: 'This is my Son, whom I love; with him I am well pleased' (Matt. 3:17). God spoke in different ways to his people: the dreams of patriarchs, the oracles of prophets, the proverbs of wise men, the priestly instruction of the law, appearances of the angel of the Lord. But the voice from heaven had pride of place. Jews called it the 'daughter of the Voice' and revered it intensely. What the voice said on that occasion was gripping: Jesus was God's Son. God loved him. God was delighted with him.

   The statement recalled two Old Testament utterances about the Messiah. First, there was Psalm 2:7: 'You are my Son; today I have become your Father'— the Messiah was God's Son whom he loved. Secondly, it recalled Isaiah 42:1: 'Here is my servant, whom I uphold, my chosen one in whom I delight' — the Messiah was God's Servant in whom he took delight. When John baptized Jesus in Jordan, the voice from heaven affirmed Jesus to be God's Son, the anointed Servant of the Lord.

His death

The transfiguration of Jesus focuses on the death of Christ as Son of God. Again, the voice from heaven is heard but this time there is an added dimension: 'This is my Son, whom I love; with him I am well pleased. Listen to him!' (Matt. 17:5). The addition recalls Deuteronomy 18:15: 'The Lord your God will raise up for you a prophet like me from among your own brothers. You must listen to him' — the Messiah was God's prophet who must be heeded. Psalms, Prophets and Law were combining to affirm Jesus as God's Son, the King, Priest and Prophet of God's appointment.

The transfiguration emphasizes Jesus' greatness as the divine Son of God. The aura of brightness around him stresses his deity. Jesus speaks with Moses and Elijah. God's Son talks with representative figures of the Law and the Prophets. But there is also a focus on Jesus' death in all this. The transfiguration occurs six days after Peter confesses Jesus as Messiah, as Jesus begins to instruct his disciples on the necessity of his death (Mark 8:31; 9:12). Moses and Elijah speak with Jesus about his 'exodus', or 'departure', which he is about to bring to fulfilment at Jerusalem (Luke 9:31). The transfiguration is the occasion when Christ's sonship is declared and it is declared as anticipating his death.

His resurrection

The proclamation of Jesus highlights the resurrection of Christ as Son of God. In Antioch in Pisidia, Paul recounts the history of God's people in a sermon of promise and fulfilment. God's choice of his people, their blessings in Egypt, their inheritance of Canaan and their leadership under judges and kings eventually lead to David, a man after God's own heart, who would do everything God wanted him to do (Acts 13:22). The fulfilment of all this is in Jesus of Nazareth, announced by John the Baptist, condemned to death by the people of Jerusalem but raised to life by God:

> 'We tell you the good news: What God promised our fathers he has fulfilled for us, their children, by raising up Jesus. As it is written in the second Psalm:
>
> '"You are my Son;
> today I have become your Father"'
>
> (Acts 13:32-33).

Jesus' resurrection marks God's divine approval of his Son.

His deity

The revelation of Jesus stresses the deity of Christ's sonship. If Paul shows the glory of Christ's sonship in his resurrection, the writer to the Hebrews portrays the manifestation of Christ's sonship in his deity. Superiority is the key word here. Jesus is superior to angels, to Moses, to the Aaronic priesthood, to the entire old dispensation, for he is the mediator of a new and better covenant. Jesus' deity is the ground of his superiority. He is superior in revelation, God's full and final disclosure transcending the prophets. He is superior in providence, upholding all things by his powerful word. He is superior in redemption, providing purification for sins, and is now seated at the right hand of God (Heb. 1:1-3).

> 'So he became as much superior to the angels as the name he
> has inherited is superior to theirs. For to which of the angels
> did God ever say,

>> '"You are my Son;
>> today I have become your Father"?'
>>   (Heb. 1:4-5).

For the writer to the Hebrews, Psalm 2:7 marks the climax of Jesus' divine sonship. The writer goes on to highlight the substance of this sonship in a chain of Old Testament quotations, most of which come from the Psalms. Jesus is the divine King whose authority rests on the oath of God (Heb. 1:5; cf. 2 Sam. 7:14). Jesus is the divine Bridegroom anointed with oil above his companions (Heb. 1:8-9; cf. Ps. 45:6-7). Jesus is the divine Creator whose years will never end (Heb. 1:10-12; cf. Ps. 102:25-27). Jesus is the divine Priest whose ministry is unique (Heb. 1:13; cf. Ps. 110:1). Christ's sonship, lying at the heart of all this, explains both his deity and his superiority.

His humanity

The priesthood of Jesus draws attention to the humanity of the Son of God. For the writer to the Hebrews, as for all the New Testament witnesses, Jesus is not only divine, he is also human. This humanity has far-reaching implications for Jesus' priesthood. Every priest is selected from among men to represent them in matters related to God. Being human, the priest can deal gently with the wayward for he himself is subject to weakness. But it is not self-selection, the priest is called of God (Heb. 5:1-4).

'So Christ also did not take upon himself the glory of becoming a high priest. But God said to him,

'"You are my Son;
     today I have become your Father."

'And he says in another place,

"You are a priest for ever,
     in the order of Melchizedek"'

(Heb. 5:5-6).

Jesus fulfils both aspects of priesthood, for he is the God-man, divine and human. As God, he is perfectly equipped to represent man before God. As man, he is well able to sympathize and deal gently with man's human condition. 'Although he was a son, he learned obedience from what he suffered and, once made perfect, he became the source of eternal salvation for all who obey him and was designated by God to be high priest in the order of Melchizedek' (Heb. 5:8-10). Jesus' priesthood, which arises from his deity as Son, combines with a humanity which tenderly and effectively cares for his people. Jesus' priesthood stresses the humanity of the Son of God.

In all of these references to Christ's enthronement from Psalm 2:7, the authority of Jesus, as Son of God, is evident. The baptism, death, resurrection, deity and humanity of Christ all emphasize the authority of this sonship. But it is an authority which has its practical outworkings in the word of the gospel of which Jesus is the essence. Jesus is the enthroned King, whose sonship must underlie the church's proclamation.

The Revival of 1859 engulfed Ulster in titanic blessing. It came to be known as 'the year of grace'. It was God's river in spate. There was a suddenness about it all. From the prayers of four believers in a little schoolhouse in Kells the flame spread with speed to our village of Ahoghill and thence throughout the province. Hundreds stood in pouring rain in the Diamond in Ahoghill to hear the gospel. Hundreds were suddenly swept into the kingdom of God both there and elsewhere. Then the flame died down and God's river returned to its former rate of flow.

Immediate as it was, it was not without preparatory signs. In the early years of the nineteenth century, there had been a vigorous theological battle. Arianism, led by Rev. Henry Montgomery, decrying the deity of Jesus, had again reared its ugly head. The Rev. Henry Cooke, the champion of orthodoxy, effectively defeated this heretical strain and the truth of Jesus the God-man gained the day. Christ was proclaimed from Scripture as the Son of God, both divine and human. From that point onwards, the cause of biblical Christianity began to flourish quite significantly. The ground was cleared for an effective outpouring of the Spirit by the vindication of Jesus, the enthroned Son of the living God. The revival was not only preceded by earnest prayer but by doctrinal preaching about Jesus as Son of God.

Evangelism today has suffered a crisis of credibility, not only because of method but also because of the substance of the message. Another gospel can so easily arise which looks like the authentic gospel but the biblical Christ is not at the centre of it. The enthroned king of the second psalm proclaimed with power in the glory of his sonship in the New Testament had these amazing effects. Only when we recover this kind of proclamation, both in promise and fulfilment, will we do justice to such a great salvation.

His headship

The anointing of the king of Psalm 2 is fulfilled in the lordship of Christ, the enthronement in his sonship and the empowering in his headship. Here, in this last, the focus is on verse 9 of the psalm:

'You will rule them with an iron sceptre;
    you will dash them to pieces like pottery.'

There are three references to this verse in the book of Revelation (Rev. 2:27; 12:5; 19:15). All three point to Christ's headship over the church. As King of the church, Christ wields his iron sceptre and dashes his enemies to pieces like a piece of pottery. The scene of these activities is both on earth and in heaven. Christ's headship through his iron sceptre is both on behalf of the church militant, as she struggles with problems and opposition here and now, and for his church triumphant as she shares his victory in heaven hereafter.

A church in difficulty

In Revelation 2:27 the headship of Christ is *projected to* the church at Thyatira. The church at Thyatira had much to commend it. But sadly it tolerated Jezebel, a self-styled prophetess, who misled the believers into sexual immorality and the eating of food sacrificed to idols. This was no doubt their involvement in the guild banquets, where their presence was a virtual necessity for success in business. Compromise with the world was eating out the heart of the church at Thyatira.

The problem, however, was even more complex than that. Jezebel appears to have been suggesting to the Christians a policy of collusion with the world around them. Believers, she taught, must learn 'Satan's so-called deep secrets' if they are to come to terms with their problems (Rev. 2:24). This is a frequent ploy today. We are told that we must experience sin to be able to understand it and to come to terms with it. Flirting with, rather than fleeing from, temptation is the suggested course of action.

To a policy of compromise and collusion, Christ responds with a blunt command for confrontation: 'Now I say to the rest of you in Thyatira, to you who do not hold to her teaching and have not learned Satan's so-called deep secrets (I will not impose any other burden on you): Only hold on to what you have until I come' (Rev. 2:24-25). The Christians are to resist all Jezebel's suggestions. Friendship with the world means enmity towards God.

The motivation which Christ gives for this confrontation is a strong one. It is not simply his own headship over all things that will ensure Jezebel's destruction but a headship which Christ gives to his church. Christ the King empowers them with his own authority to confront the enemy, and this authority derives from the prophecy of Psalm 2. Christ gives to his people his iron sceptre to wield against their foes:

'To him who overcomes and does my will to the end, I will
give authority over the nations—

"'He will rule them with an iron sceptre;
    he will dash them to pieces like pottery"'—

'just as I have received authority from my Father. I will also
give him the morning star. He who has an ear, let him hear
what the Spirit says to the churches'

                                                        (Rev. 2:26-29).

A woman and her child

In Revelation 12:5 the headship of Christ is *protected for* the church.
I remember as a boy standing looking at an image of a lady, her head
surrounded by what looked like twelve light bulbs. It was a strange
sight to my eyes, a mixture of ancient and modern, an alien culture
to my own. When, later, I read Revelation 12, it became clearer to
me: 'a woman clothed with the sun, with the moon under her feet and
a crown of twelve stars on her head' (Rev. 12:1). The image was of
the Virgin Mary, supposedly the mother of the male child in
Revelation 12.

Revelation 12 presents a vision of a woman and her child, who
are miraculously protected. Initially in the vision, the woman is
pregnant and is confronted by an immense dragon with seven
heads. The dragon is waiting for the woman to give birth and then
will devour the child. The woman gives birth, and a baby boy is
born. Before the dragon strikes, the child is snatched away to God
and his throne. The woman flees to the desert, there to be cared for
by God.

The protection continues, not just from the dragon but from two
ferocious beasts. Michael and the angels fight with the dragon in
heaven and cast him down to earth. The dragon pursues the woman
but she is given wings and flies away. The dragon spews out water
to engulf her but the earth swallows up the deluge. A beast later
comes from the sea and one from the earth to assist the dragon.
Ultimately, the Lamb — the child now a man — with his followers,
destroys this horrendous enemy and they rejoice in triumph. What
does all this mean?

Biblically speaking, it is the story of the struggle between the seed of the woman, mankind, and the seed of the serpent, the devil. The woman is not so much the Virgin Mary as the people of God; the child is Christ; the dragon represents Satan. The story repeats itself, stage by stage, through Old Testament history until the coming of Christ, the male child in the vision. Revelation rescreens the final stage in the drama. Christ, protected from birth, eventually triumphs over Satan on behalf of his people, the church.

The description of the child is startling. It brings us back to Psalm 2:9, to the empowering of Christ in his headship for the church: 'She gave birth to a son, a male child, who will rule all the nations with an iron sceptre. And her child was snatched up to God and to his throne' (Rev. 12:5).

God guards the power of Christ from infancy, so that ultimately he may rule universally. God protects both the empowered Christ and his victorious church.

A rider on a white horse

In Revelation 19:15 the headship of Christ is *perfected in* the church. The film was called *The Rider on the Pale Horse*. It was a western. It began, as usual, with the cowboy riding into town. He came from a distance but as he got closer his horse was pale and he was dressed in black buckskin from head to foot. The music of the soundtrack faded and a little girl in the homestead read words from Revelation as she watched the rider approach: 'When the Lamb opened the fourth seal, I heard the voice of the fourth living creature say, "Come!" I looked, and there before me was a pale horse! Its rider was named Death, and Hades was following close behind him. They were given power over a fourth of the earth to kill by sword, famine and plague, and by the wild beasts of the earth' (Rev. 6:7-8). As the plot unfolded the rider wreaked vengeance on a group of gunmen who had wronged him in the past. I never forgot that introduction. It burned the truth of Revelation into my mind.

The story of the horseman in Revelation 19 is markedly different from that of Revelation 6. The rider is on a white, not a pale horse. He rides in the glory of leadership. Death and hell are replaced by life and heaven. Vengeance towards his enemies is matched by forgiveness for his friends. Above all, victory is in the air. The armies of heaven are following him, riding on white horses and dressed in fine linen, white and clean. He captures and destroys the beast and the false prophet. He does this as the empowered Christ of the second psalm. 'Out of his mouth comes a sharp sword with which to strike down the nations. "He will rule them with an iron sceptre." He treads the winepress of the fury of the wrath of God Almighty' (Rev. 19:15).

The headship of Christ is here in ultimate triumph. The child, now a man, is victorious. His victory is universal. His enemies are totally defeated. He is King of kings and Lord of lords (Rev. 19:16). The story is now complete. Christ's headship, projected to the church and protected for the church, is now perfected in the church. The power is again that of the iron sceptre. By it, Christ wields his authority, governing his friends and destroying his foes. The empowering of the king stands fulfilled in Christ's headship over all things but, above all, on behalf of his church. The church, militant and triumphant, rejoices in the iron sceptre of the king of the second psalm. The church enjoys both the protection and the victory of Christ's headship.

All these truths come from the king of the second psalm, an anointed king whose lordship inspires his people to prayer in times of desperate need, an enthroned king whose sonship underlies his word of gospel proclamation and an empowered king whose headship governs the church on earth and in heaven. Christ's kingship helps believers in prayer, in the Word, in daily living and leads them eventually to victory in glory. David's anointed, enthroned and empowered king is great David's greater Son, Jesus Christ, King of kings and Lord of lords. The New Testament references to Psalm 2 make this abundantly clear.

> All hail the power of Jesus' name!
> Let angels prostrate fall;
> Bring forth the royal diadem,
> To crown him Lord of all.
>
> Crown him, ye martyrs of your God,
> Who from his altar call;
> Extol him in whose path ye trod,
> And crown him Lord of all.

Ye seed of Israel's chosen race,
Ye ransomed of the Fall,
Hail him who saves you by his grace,
And crown him Lord of all.

Sinners, whose love can ne'er forget
The wormwood and the gall,
Go, spread your trophies at his feet,
And crown him Lord of all.

Let every tongue and every tribe,
Responsive to the call,
To him all majesty ascribe,
And crown him Lord of all.

O that, with yonder sacred throng,
We at his feet may fall,
Join in the everlasting song,
And crown him Lord of all!

(Edward Perronet)

2.
Second Adam

Psalm 8 depicts man as the crown of God's creation both in humiliation and exaltation. David is overwhelmed by the glory of God in the world around him. God's being is written large on everything David sees. His majestic name is evident throughout the earth. His magnificence overarches the heavens. Space is his design work. Planets and luminaries he sets into place with exquisite and orderly craftsmanship. The entire scene reflects God as Creator with impressive and breathtaking effect. It is the work, too, not of a remote deity who plans out of mere self-satisfaction, but of a God David can relate to as his, and his people's, God. That adds particular lustre to God's creatorhood.

Man in humiliation

Man is so small in all this creation. He is infinitesimal, a mere speck on a speck. This grips David's mind. How does God even notice man among all the things he has created? What moves God to care for man in his littleness amid all the largeness of his creation? For God to notice man is remarkable; that he should care for him, incomprehensible. Yet God does even more than that. Man is made in a low condition, a nonentity in terms of size, amid the grandeur of God's handiwork. Yet man is uniquely made. He is made 'a little lower than the heavenly beings and crowned ... with glory and honour' (Ps. 8:5). The full force of this rocks David's contemplations. The word he uses, translated 'heavenly beings', is the Hebrew *Elohim*, which is one of the Old Testament names for 'God'. David is saying that man's condition is nothing less than the divine and celestial state. Man is godlike as he leaves the Creator's hands. In this he stands unique amid all God's creation.

> 'O Lord, our Lord
>> how majestic is your name in all the earth!
> You have set your glory
>> above the heavens.
> From the lips of children and infants
>> you have ordained praise
> because of your enemies,
>> to silence the foe and the avenger.
> When I consider your heavens,
>> the work of your fingers,
> the moon and the stars,
>> which you have set in place,
> what is man that you are mindful of him,
>> the son of man that you care for him?
> You made him a little lower than the heavenly beings
>> and crowned him with glory and honour'
>
>> (Ps. 8:1-5).

Behind David's meditations lies the creation story of Genesis. Adam, along with Eve, was made in a low yet unique condition. God, who called all things into being by his word of command, is the glory behind Psalm 8. The stately procession of creation — light, water, sky, land, vegetation, sun, moon, birds, fish, animals — from greater to lesser, underlies David's thoughts. Man, in all this, is the tail-piece. Yet Moses, with David, stresses man's unique state. The beasts of the field and the birds of the air were formed out of the ground (Gen. 2:19). God, indeed, formed man from the dust of the earth but breathed into his nostrils the breath of life. Man became a living being (Gen. 2:7). More than that, it was the divine decision to create man as unique:

> 'Let us make man in our image, in our likeness . . .
> So God created man
>> in his own image,
> in the image of God
>> he created him;

male and female
he created them'

(Gen. 1:26-27).

Man was created with an affinity to God. There was a marked difference between man and the creatures. Whether we set this simply at the level of man's lordship over the creatures, or his superior intelligence as compared with them, or as some spiritual potential within man to relate to and to communicate with God, man was clearly different. David and Moses both recognize this. The first Adam was created in a low but unique condition, 'made ... a little lower than the heavenly beings ... crowned ... with glory and honour' (Ps. 8:5).

Man's low but unique condition strikes me each time I travel by air. As the plane soars into the sky, above is the glory of the heavens; all around are the tokens of God's handiwork — the rolling hills, the ridged sea, the pleasant planet earth; beneath, etched into the green fields, are the geometric designs of man's creation — the lineal roads, the matchbox cars, the rising blocks of varied buildings, square, rectangular and domed. God's and man's work stand alongside each other, different yet complementary. There is a strange link between them: the grandeur and majesty of the divine reflected in the intelligence and order of the human. When we relax near a favourite little resort, the same thought occurs: the uncontrollable sea, sometimes calm, sometimes rough, the jutting promontory rocks, rugged yet beautiful, the shops and hotels bustling with people, the new marina with the children playing — God's work and man's side by side, man's low by comparison yet unique in individuality.

How glorious is God's image in his creature man! God's goodness 'in common grace' ensures this. Common grace describes God's favour to all his creatures, good or evil, caring for them in providence and love. Special grace is specifically God's action in Christ, saving sinners from sin. In common grace the Lord is good to all. He provides for man and beast. He makes his sun to shine on the just and unjust. More than that, God's creativity rubs off on man. Man writes symphonies and paints masterpieces. He splits the atom and reconstructs shattered limbs. He designs computers and pens poems. Man is even capable of goodness to his fellow-man, a reflection of the Creator's good to mankind. Yet, in all of God's creation, man is so small, so infinitesimal.

But there is another side to man's humiliation, a side which David clearly knows and which Moses emphasizes. Man, made a little lower than the heavenly beings and crowned with glory, is yet a fallen creature. His glory is dreadfully marred. Only the vestiges of the divine image remain. Man harms, kills, wounds, deceives and betrays his fellow-man. Adam, as he left his Creator's hand was perfect — low yet unique. Now man is distorted, disfigured, shamed by sin. His glory is fatally clouded. Only a 'second Adam' can resolve his plight.

Man in exaltation

Psalm 8 speaks of man as the crown of God's creation, not only in humiliation but also in exaltation. We have already seen part of that exaltation, even in his low state of humiliation. It is evident in his uniqueness. David goes on to specify man's exaltation in one aspect of this uniqueness in particular, his lordship over the creatures. God has appointed man as curator over the world in which he has placed him. Man is God's vicegerent on earth and over earth. That is his crowning glory.

'You made him a little lower than the heavenly beings
    and crowned him with glory and honour.
You made him ruler over the works of your hands;
    you put everything under his feet:
all flocks and herds,
    and the beasts of the field,
the birds of the air,
    and the fish of the sea,
    and all that swim the paths of the seas.
O Lord, our Lord,
    how majestic is your name in all the earth!'

                (Ps. 8:5-9).

My earliest recollection of these words is standing with my parents singing them in church to the metrical version of the psalm:

Lord of thy works thou hast him made:
All unto him must yield,

All sheep and oxen, yea, and beasts
Which roam the field,

Fowl of the air, fish of the sea,
All that pass through the same.
O Lord our Lord, in all the earth
How great thy name!

Even as a boy, I thrilled at the dignity of man's place in the world.
I could see the different breeds and colours of birds, the shining
scales of herring, the mammoth proportions of whale and dolphin,
the cows and sheep in the fields, the lions and leopards in the jungle
— and over them all was man, lord by God's appointment. What a
privilege! What a responsibility!

Behind the description of the psalm lie the definitions of Genesis.
Both David's poem and Moses' words point in the same direction.
God placed Adam in a garden, rich in mineral wealth and fruitful in
plant life. God gave Adam the task of caring for the land. The fruit
and vegetation were his for the taking. God presented the creatures
to Adam so that he might name them and, in a very real way, declare
his possession of them and his lordship over them. The express
intention of the divine decision to create man was with a view to
man's lordship over the creatures. Then God said, 'Let us make man
in our image, in our likeness, and let them rule over the fish of the
sea and the birds of the air, over the livestock, over all the earth and
over all the creatures that move along the ground' (Gen. 1:26).
Man's curatorship over the earth is by divine appointment.

This privilege and responsibility persist throughout Scripture.
The creation ordinances to increase, to work, to care and to rule are
fleshed out in the details given in the covenant with Noah and in the
law on Sinai. These set the parameters of our curatorship. The
'Green people' are right in this aspect of their emphasis. Care of
planet Earth, and of all within it, is a privilege and responsibility
imposed by God on man. Not only care for the starving multitudes,
rejection of cruelty to the oppressed, protection of the weak,
children and animals, but problems of abortion, euthanasia, divorce,
genetic engineering, pollution and conservation should always have
a place on the Christian agenda. We are responsible to God for our
world and for all within it. Green philosophy is wrong, however, in
that it regards the planet Earth as an end in itself or, where it does

recognize God, it sees man purely as a creature on the planet with no account for his fallen nature or sinful condition. It has no moral context. It is amoral and so biblically defective.

Ron Elsdon, in *Green House Theology — Biblical Perspectives on Caring for Creation*, has helpfully pitched the debate within its scriptural context, rather than within the Green philosophy or New Age thinking. As evangelicals, we do well to take his advice seriously: 'If the God of the Bible really is concerned about our care of his creation, that theme should be there throughout, from Genesis to Revelation. More than that, it should be possible to trace this concern in a coherent way, as a continuous thread running right through the history of the Creator's dealing with his world ... it should be possible to uncover a fundamental link with the gospel itself. I believe I have been able to find and trace this thread. I can even give it a name: the goodness of creation.'

The Fall, however, mars this goodness and the pinnacle of man's privilege and responsibility. His curatorship of the world is also vitiated by his depravity: Adam's exalted rôle became well-nigh impossible because he sinned. The ground was cursed because of his sin. He struggled with thorns and thistles as he hoed and planted. From the sweat of his brow he ate the produce of the land. The land, from which he had originally come, eventually swallowed him up. Dust he was; to dust he returned.

The whole creation continues groaning in pain, along with Adam, excluded as he was from the glory of Eden. We cage the wild beasts, or they tear us to pieces. Nature is 'red in tooth and claw'. The lion lying down with the lamb and the child's hand in the snake's nest is a future hope, not a present reality. Not only the uniqueness of man's humiliation, but the vicegerency of his exaltation is soured by sin. A 'second Adam' is needed here also. But Ron Elsdon is right. There is a continuous thread, a fundamental link, between the Creator's dealing with his world and the gospel itself. In the mercy of God, there was not only a first but a second Adam, the 'second man', the 'last Adam', the Lord Jesus Christ.

Christ in restoration

Christ is presented forcefully in the New Testament as the Second Adam, for while the actual term is not used, the 'second man' and the 'last Adam' express the same view (1 Cor. 15:45,47). Related to this theme of the Second Adam is the pattern of Christ's humiliation and exaltation, his incarnation and death, resurrection and ascension. The Psalms make their own distinctive contribution in the New Testament to the saga of this dying and risen Messiah. Quoting from Psalm 8, the writer to the Hebrews speaks of Christ's humiliation as the Second Adam, low yet unique in his dignified condition (Heb. 2:5-18). From the same psalm, Paul stresses Christ's exaltation as the Second Adam, his lordship, as God's regent, over things both physical and spiritual (1 Cor. 15:20-28). Both apostles source their ideas quite specifically in Psalm 8. This psalm, which speaks of the first Adam, is fulfilled in Christ, the Second Adam.

The writer to the Hebrews begins his letter by painting an impressive picture of Jesus as the divine Son of God (Heb. 1). In this, the Psalms have a conspicuous part to play. Echoes of the Psalms resound to the glory of Jesus as Son, King, Bridegroom and Creator. It is for this very reason that his readers must pay careful attention to what they have heard so that they do not drift away (Heb. 1:1-2:4).

Jesus is not only divine, however, he is also human. This is a staggering truth, but one which is not purely academic. It has very practical implications. Jesus is the God-man, high enough to represent God before man, low enough to represent man before God. But how is Jesus human? The writer explains by quoting Psalm 8 :

'It is not to angels that he has subjected the world to come, about which we are speaking. But there is a place where someone has testified:

"What is man that you are mindful of him,
   the son of man that you care for him?
You made him a little lower than the angels;
   you crowned him with glory and honour
   and put everything under his feet."

'In putting everything under him, God left nothing that is not subject to him. Yet at present we do not see everything subject to him. But we see Jesus, who was made a little lower than the angels, now crowned with glory and honour because he suffered death, so that by the grace of God he might taste death for everyone'

(Heb. 2:5-9).

A low condition

The writer specifies Christ's low condition from Psalm 8. Jesus, as man, was made a little lower than the angels. This is the writer's continuing theme. He traces the thread of Jesus' humanity through his entire life and work. It was fitting that God should make the author of man's salvation perfect through suffering (Heb. 2:10). Both the one who makes men holy and those who are made holy are of the same family. Jesus is not ashamed to call them brothers (Heb. 2:11). Since the children shared flesh and blood, he too shared in their humanity (Heb. 2:14). It is not angels he helps but Abraham's descendants (Heb. 2:16). For this reason he had to be made like his brothers in every way (Heb. 2:17).

Christ's incarnation is clearly before us here. The fact of Jehovah becoming flesh in the person of Jesus is the telling truth which the writer to the Hebrews describes. What John said of the Word becoming flesh and Paul of Jesus being made of a woman, made under the law, the apostle to the Hebrews describes as a family likeness, a common humanity, fitting God's purpose of salvation down to the very details of suffering and death. This is the Second Adam's low condition. Jesus' state of humiliation is his incarnation and, thence, his suffering and his death. In that sense, he was made 'a little lower than the angels'.

A unique condition

The uniqueness of Jesus' low condition grips the apostle's mind just as it did the psalmist's. Jesus is seen not only as made a little lower than the angels, but as 'crowned with glory and honour'. But how is Jesus crowned with glory and honour? Had the writer identified this as Christ's human state in Adam — godlike, after God's image and likeness — we would have expected it. Had he enlarged on the contrast and stressed the wonder of Christ's condition as actually both God and man, the God-man, we would have been amazed at it. But how does the writer describe the uniqueness of Jesus' *low* condition? He relates it to Jesus' death! He specifies the horror of

Calvary as the crowning glory of Jesus' life and work. Christ's humiliation, above all, stands evident in this — that he died! It is something, too, that has already taken place: he is 'now crowned with glory and honour' (Heb. 2:9). It has immeasurably practical implications: 'so that by the grace of God he might taste death for everyone' (Heb. 2:9). At this we simply stagger.

This means that the uniqueness of the Second Adam's low condition is located in his death and it is related also to his condition of exaltation. The writer to the Hebrews develops this thought alongside the theme of Christ's humanity (Heb. 2:14-18). The ultimate purpose of Christ's humanity finds fulfilment in his death. This death is the death of the Second Adam. By his death, in this low yet unique condition, the Second Adam resolves the disastrous situation left by the first Adam. Christ comes and dies to remove man's plight by restoring man to the primal image in which God created him. The remarkable thing is that the writer attributes to the Second Adam success in those very areas where the first Adam failed.

Redemption

Christ, the Second Adam, restores by redeeming man from sin. 'Since the children have flesh and blood, he too shared in their humanity so that by his death he might destroy him who holds the power of death — that is, the devil — and free those who all their lives were held in slavery by their fear of death' (Heb. 2:14-15). Death for the first Adam marked the judgement of God on his fallen condition. The work of the Second Adam takes up the theme at the precise point of the first Adam's failure. The Second Adam's death marks not the curse of God, but the blessing of God. Christ's death becomes the gateway to life. It brings relief from judgement and destruction by the devil. It promises redemption from the enslaving, separating and deadening power of sin.

Atonement

Christ, the Second Adam, restores by atoning for sin. 'For this reason he had to be made like his brothers in every way, in order that he might become a merciful and faithful high priest in service to

God, and that he might make atonement for the sins of the people' (Heb. 2:17). The root-idea behind the Hebrew word for atonement is 'covering', a covering over of sin from the just and wrathful gaze of God. When Adam and Eve sinned, their eyes were opened to evil. They viewed their nakedness with shame, sewed fig leaves together and made coverings for themselves. Shame, because of sin, not only drove them to hide from one another, but from God. God later made garments of skin for Adam and Eve and clothed them. Even in judgement, God was merciful. God's mercy persists in his judgement and, through the Second Adam, God provides a perfect covering for man's sin. His shame is removed. His guilt is erased. His crime is expiated. His sin is atoned for.

Salvation

Christ, the Second Adam, restores by saving from sin. 'Because he himself suffered when he was tempted, he is able to help those who are being tempted' (Heb. 2:18). Here, the specific emphasis of salvation is deliverance from temptation. Adam and Eve fell because they could not resist the temptation to eat the forbidden fruit. The Second Adam comes to deliver from that situation. Faced by the drawing deceit of Satan, man when tempted is helped by Christ. Christ's supreme power as Son of God means that he can deliver those who are tempted.

The persistent note of the writer to the Hebrews is that, at the precise points where the first Adam failed, the Second Adam succeeds. The Second Adam, in his low yet unique condition of incarnation and death, provides redemption, atonement and salvation, where the first Adam was powerless. Christ, in his humiliation 'made a little lower than the angels', is 'now crowned with glory and honour because he suffered death'. Christ releases man from the awful entail of that death; Adam was hopeless and trapped. The work of the Second Adam is supremely that of restoration at the precise point where it is needed.

Daniel did some missionary work in Malawi. He was a builder by trade. Among his duties was repair work on a cathedral church which had been damaged. Years later, an Anglican bishop wrote to me in glowing terms of his work. The amount of time and expertise my friend had spent on the work was quite obvious: the assessment of the damage, the viability of restoration, the materials needed, the matching of the new to the old. The most striking thing, the bishop wrote, was the finished work. When completed, it was virtually impossible to tell where the repairs had been made. They were so well moulded into the original. The dignity and beauty of the first creation were retained. The damaged features were totally erased. Repairs had been effected exactly where they were needed. It was a classic work of restoration.

The Second Adam restores men's lives like that. It is not a mere cosmetic exercise to cover over the cracks and give the appearance of soundness. Christ assesses exactly the extent of the damage, gauges with precision what is needed and restores man in salvation so that the original lines of the Creator's design are fulfilled to perfection. Christ meets man precisely at the point of need and effects restoration there. Redemption, atonement, salvation, righteousness, holiness, knowledge, are all involved. It is a classic work of restoration too, effected through Christ the Second Adam in his humiliation, low yet unique, doing what the first Adam was powerless to do. The writer to the Hebrews gains this perception from Psalm 8. 'But we see Jesus, who was made a little lower than the angels, now crowned with glory and honour because he suffered death, so that by the grace of God he might taste death for everyone' (Heb. 2:9).

> O loving wisdom of our God!
> When all was sin and shame,
> A second Adam to the fight
> And to the rescue came.
>
> O wisest love! that flesh and blood
> Which did in Adam fail
> Should strive afresh against the foe
> Should strive and should prevail;
>
> O generous love! that he who smote
> In man, for man, the foe
> The double agony in man
> For man, should undergo.

> (J. H. Newman)

Christ in regeneration

Paul, from Psalm 8, emphasizes Christ's exaltation, his lordship as Second Adam over things natural and spiritual (1 Cor. 15:20-28). The church at Corinth abounded in problems: party divisions, incest, Christians taking one another to law, disorder in public worship, abuse of spiritual gifts and, to crown it all, questions over resurrection. Of course, the classic problem in Greek society for Christian teaching was not a flat denial of the afterlife, but a belief in the immortality of the soul over against the resurrection of the body. To Greeks the idea of bodily resurrection was a nonsense. It was strange, though, that this should pervade Corinth, the promiscuous seaport. At Athens, the cultural centre, one would have expected it, but not at Corinth. Yet at Corinth it was there, among all the other problems.

Paul meets this problem with startling clarity (1 Cor. 15:1-58). The resurrection of Christ is basic Christian belief. This is because it is historic fact. Christ not only died but rose again according to the Scriptures. He appeared not only to individuals but to over five hundred brothers at the same time. It was no hallucination. How then can people deny bodily resurrection if Christ rose from the dead? If Christ did not rise from the dead, Christian preaching is pernicious, Christian faith is fictitious and Christians are liars.

Christ did, however, rise from death and Christ's resurrection implies the resurrection of the dead. At this point Adam/Christ imagery enters Paul's argument and, with it, the exalted 'man' of Psalm 8: 'But Christ has indeed been raised from the dead, the firstfruits of those who have fallen asleep. For since death came through a man, the resurrection of the dead comes also through a man. For as in Adam all die, so in Christ all will be made alive. But each in his own turn: Christ, the firstfruits; then, when he comes, those who belong to him. Then the end will come, when he hands over the kingdom to God the Father after he has destroyed all dominion, authority and power. For he must reign until he has put all his enemies under his feet. The last enemy to be destroyed is death. For he "has put everything under his feet". Now when it says that "everything" has been put under him, it is clear that this does not include God himself, who put everything under Christ. When he has done this, then the Son himself will be made subject to him who put everything under him, so that God may be all in all' (1 Cor. 15:20-28).

A successful work

The work of the Second Adam, in contrast to that of the first Adam, is eminently successful. Just as the first Adam was appointed as God's curator of the created world and responsible to God for it, so the Second Adam is appointed as God's regent over all things so that in due course, as a responsible steward, he might hand over all to God. 'When he has done this, then the Son himself will be made subject to him who put everything under him, so that God may be all in all' (1 Cor. 15:28). Paul, reflecting on man's appointed lordship over creation in Psalm 8, which in the event proved a failed exercise, rejoices in the lordship of Christ as Second Adam over all things, which is proving, and will ultimately prove, a glorious success. The lordship of the Second Adam is sovereign, ordered and triumphant, just as that of the first Adam was defective, distorted and ultimately destroyed.

Regencies have always played an important part in rule down through history. Whether it was the Candace or queen mother of ancient Ethiopia, the dauphin of France, the governors of the young Edward of England, or even the leaders during the interregnum under Cromwell, deputed responsible authority has been a way of government. The 'deputed' nature of the office does not detract from the power or authority of the deputy. Being God's 'Regent', Christ is not robbed of his divine sonship; his equality within the Godhead is not infringed. The point here is that Christ, as the perfect man, the Second Adam, exercises the function of deputed rule. This accords both with his person as eternal Son and with his work as anointed man. Calvin puts it well: 'Farther, it must be observed, that he has been appointed Lord and highest King, so as to be as it were the Father's Vicegerent in the government of the world ... that we may not think that there is any other governor, lord, protector, or judge of the dead and living but may fix our contemplation on him alone... But Christ will then restore the kingdom which he has received, that we may cleave wholly to God. Nor will he in this way resign the kingdom but will transfer it in a manner from his humanity to his glorious divinity ... and Christ's humanity will then no longer be interposed to keep us back from a closer view to God.' This exciting view of Christ's lordship arises from Psalm 8. Christ acts as vicegerent or deputy of God.

A spiritual work

The work of the Second Adam is not only ordered; it is markedly spiritual. The lordship of Christ in exaltation extends not only over the natural, but over the spiritual world as well. Indeed, it is in this that the success of the Second Adam over against the failure of the first Adam is most clearly seen. Here, the similarity of Adam with Christ, in terms of responsible lordship as curator or vicegerent of God, ceases. There follows a marked contrast, an essential difference, between the work of the first and that of the Second Adam. Adam's responsibility over the natural world, flawed by the Fall, ends in sin and destruction. Christ's perfect regency, over both natural and spiritual worlds, results in glory and triumph.

New life

Christ's lordship is spiritual, for in himself resides spiritual life. A new life is the inevitable result. 'But Christ has ... been raised from the dead, the firstfruits of those who have fallen asleep' (1 Cor. 15:20). The 'firstfruits' were the first gleanings of a new harvest. They were presented to God in the temple, for they were holy to the Lord. They marked the promise of a future harvest, more of the same order. Christ's uniqueness is in view here. Elsewhere, Paul describes Christ as the 'firstborn from among the dead', the prototype of a new species. The first Adam succumbed to death as the wages of sin. The Second Adam destroys death and triumphs in righteousness over it, for the last enemy to be destroyed is death. Christ, as 'firstfruits', produces a harvest of those who have his new life within them.

New rule

Christ's lordship is spiritual, for he administers spiritual rule. A new rule is established. 'Then the end will come, when he hands over the kingdom to God the Father after he has destroyed all dominion, authority and power. For he must reign until he has put all enemies under his feet' (1 Cor. 15:24-25). Paul here stresses all power and authority, evil and good, natural and spiritual. The first Adam, because of the Fall, handed the kingdom over to the devil. The Second Adam resists the temptation of the kingdom of this world and, ultimately, hands over the kingdom to God his Father. The kingdoms of this world become the kingdom of our Lord and of his Christ and he will reign for ever and ever. Christ's new rule takes control of the lives of his people.

New man

Christ's lordship is spiritual for he produces a spiritual offspring. A new man is born. 'So it is written: "The first man Adam became a living being"; the last Adam, a life-giving spirit... As was the earthly man, so are those who are of the earth; and as is the man from heaven, so also are those who are of heaven. And just as we have borne the likeness of the earthly man, so shall we bear the likeness of the man from heaven' (1 Cor. 15:45,48-49). Moses tells us that when God created man, he made him in the likeness of God, both male and female and, when Adam had lived 130 years, he had a son in his own likeness, in his own image, whom he named Seth (Gen. 5:1-3). Paul here recalls that when the Second Adam completes his work he produces those who bear his image, the likeness of the man from heaven. Christ is the progenitor of an entirely new order of creation. 'Therefore, if anyone is in Christ, he is a new creation; the old has gone, the new has come' (2 Cor. 5:17).

Regeneration is the only adequate term to describe this work. The exalted Christ, as Second Adam and God's Vicegerent, exercises a lordship over both natural and spiritual, which resurrects dead human nature to eternal life beyond even man's primal glory. A new life, a new rule, a new man is the result. It is restoration by means of regeneration. It is not fanning into flame the hidden spark of God in man or unveiling to full brightness the dimmed light that is in every man by creation. The restoration of the Second Adam is much more radical than that. It is resurrecting from death the fallen and twisted image of God in man. It is breathing into man's nostrils the breath of spiritual life.

An adherent member of our congregation came to faith in Christ. He had been one of the most upright, moral and kind persons I had ever known. He was the sort of man whose lifestyle, even in those early days, could have led you to believe he was already a Christian. But he was not and he knew it. Then he came to faith in Christ and a remarkable change occurred. The old morality continued, but his kindness and warmth grew in intensity as a new dimension entered his life. He started attending mid-week meetings with interest and enthusiasm. He prayed, falteringly at first, in the prayer meeting but then with growing openness and ease. He questioned me about study of the Scriptures and obviously found the Bible to be spiritual food. I could see clearly what had happened. Christ had restored him by regenerating him. The old features of common grace persisted; a new breath of special grace filled his entire life. It was a classic example of the Second Adam at work.

Ezekiel, in his valley of dry bones, had obeyed God and proclaimed his Word. The result was remarkable — a rattling, a joining, a covering — from bones to bodies. But they were lifeless, a corpselike regiment of dead soldiers strewn on a dusty battlefield. Ezekiel obeyed God again. He prayed for the breath, the wind, the Spirit to blow on them. The Hebrew word *ruach* means both 'breath' and 'spirit'. They stood up on their feet — a vast army, now resurrected to life. That is the work of the Second Adam. He restores by regenerating. In the low but unique condition of his humiliation, he restores by his incarnation and death: redeeming, atoning, saving. In his exaltation as God's vicegerent over natural and spiritual, he resurrects from death: a new life, a new rule, a new man. The dignity of creation overreaches itself in the glory of re-creation. Man soars even beyond the delights of unfallen Adam. All of this we see of Christ from Psalm 8.

Jesus shall reign where'er the sun
Does his successive journeys run;
His kingdom stretch from shore to shore,
Till moons shall wax and wane no more.

Blessings abound where'er he reigns:
The prisoner leaps to lose his chains,
The weary find eternal rest,
And all the sons of want are blest.

Where he displays his healing power
Death and the curse are known no more;
In him the tribes of Adam boast
More blessings than their father lost.

(Isaac Watts)

3.
Righteous Sufferer

Psalm 69 is a psalm of suffering. There are a number of psalms like that. Sometimes the psalmist sees himself in a bottomless pit, or parched in a desert wasteland, or engulfed in swirling waters. The details are like a recurring nightmare. Psalm 69 comes from David's experience. Perhaps it was from the time when he was hunted by Saul or distraught by Absalom's rebellion. Certain aspects of his suffering stand out. They show David's suffering to be deep and horrific.

Innocence

The details are intense and personal. David describes it in body language. Waters splash about his neck. His feet have nothing firm to stand on. His throat is dry. His eyes are out of focus. He looks for God, but all he can see around him are enemies — hundreds of enemies hunting and hounding him, so many that they are more than the hairs on his head. Is his mind giving way too? Is he becoming paranoiac, or is it all real? They poison his food. They lace his drink with sour wine.

It is the mental agony which is so difficult to handle. The fact that he can find no reason for his suffering and persecution drives him almost mad. If he could find a cause for their enmity, even some unconscious fault in his behaviour, or a quirk in his personality that they found distasteful! But there is none — no reason, no cause. It is all so unjust. The fact that he is an 'innocent' sufferer is the bottom of David's bottomless pit:

'Save me, O God,
    for the waters have come up to my neck.
I sink in the miry depths,
    where there is no foothold.
I have come into the deep waters;
    the floods engulf me.
I am worn out calling for help;
    my throat is parched.
My eyes fail,
    looking for my God.
Those who hate me without reason
    outnumber the hairs of my head;
many are my enemies without cause,
    those who seek to destroy me.
I am forced to restore
    what I did not steal'

(Ps. 69:1-4).

This experience was so like Job's: the loss of livestock was crippling; the murder of his servants shameful; the tragic deaths of his sons and daughters an unforgettable blow; the ulcerous sores the last straw. What hurt Job most, however, what was unbearable to cope with, were the nagging insinuations of his wife that God was somehow to blame — 'Curse God and die' — or the frustrating suggestions of Job's comforters that somewhere he himself was at fault. In all this, Job was painfully innocent — that was the deepest pain of all.

Godliness

In his torture, David found some little relief in the fact that he was committed to God in all this ordeal. Indeed, it was for God's sake that he was enduring the suffering. He was assured of that. He was being attacked because God was being attacked. In his grief, he was bearing the brunt of man's enmity against God. That was the only light at the end of the tunnel. That gave some semblance of rationale to his apparently causeless pain. If David was wrong in this, his situation was completely hopeless, for it was totally purposeless.

This was all he had to hold on to in his growing sense of isolation.

His brothers despised him. His family disowned him. Those he held dearest had no time for him. He was so dreadfully alone. That frustration he converted into zeal for God. God was his chiefest joy. He would endure anything for God. The more his friends abandoned his cause, the more he would abandon himself to God's cause. That passion would consume him. His righteous suffering would eventually prove his innocence.

> 'For I endure scorn for your sake,
>   and shame covers my face.
> I am a stranger to my brothers,
>   an alien to my own mother's sons;
> for zeal for your house consumes me,
>   and the insults of those who insult you fall on me'
>   (Ps. 69:7-9).

Joseph must have felt like that. His brothers regarded his dreams as arrogance, his self-professed innocence as shrewdness. They plotted against him, threw him in the desert pit, sold him to traders, covered their tracks by dipping his famous coat in blood and blaming his tragic 'death' on a ferocious beast. Joseph was so alone. Yet God was with him all the time, even in his dreams, confirming his presence to Joseph in prison, in Potiphar's house, in the palace. Joseph held on to God and God eventually turned the curse into a blessing. Joseph, too, proved his innocence and the undeserved nature of his suffering through his righteous commitment to God.

Retribution

There was purpose even in David's reactions to his suffering. David calls down, or imprecates, God's judgement on his enemies. We find this in quite a number of psalms. These imprecatory psalms have had a very bad press. Often such sentiments have been regarded simply as fitful vengeance, a personal vendetta, spiteful bad temper. Calling a curse down on your enemy falls short of Old Testament, let alone New Testament, morality. Did not Jesus teach, 'Love your enemy'?

Yet this judgement on the imprecatory psalms can be, at times, too sweeping. It is true that they reach fever pitch of temper, express fearful longings and even send shudders down the spine. Yet human reactions aside, they often show a genuine concern for God's justice not only to be seen, but to be seen to be done, and in this the right vindication of the innocent party is also evident. It is not sufficient to dismiss the imprecatory psalms as simply 'Old Testament morality', unworthy of the New Testament. When we adopt that stance we end up with two gods — a god of the Old Testament, full of fury and justice, and a god of the New Testament, full of sentiment and love; and two Bibles — an Old Testament full of law, and a New Testament full of grace.

This is just not true. Similar imprecations, as for example 'anathemas', are found in the New Testament (Gal. 1:8,9; Rev. 6:10; 18:20; 19:1-6). On the other hand, the Old Testament, equally with the New, teaches the duty of love (Lev. 19:17) and the wisdom of returning evil with good (Ps. 7:4-5; 35:12-14). Far from being fitful vengeance, the imprecations in the psalms often express the desires of a holy man, reflect a zeal for clearing God's good name and indicate a biblical moralistic realism that God's justice demands good to be commended and evil to be punished. J. R. W. Stott writes, 'I do not find it hard to imagine situations in which holy men of God do and should both cry to God for vengeance and assert their own righteousness. Since God is going to judge the impenitent, a truly godly person will desire him to do so, and that without any feelings of personal animosity.'

Be that as it may, one thing the imprecatory psalms do prove is that God can make even the wrath of man to praise him. God can make human anger the vehicle of divine purpose. We note and understand David's imprecations. They are an integral part of his suffering:

> 'They put gall in my food
>   and gave me vinegar for my thirst.
> May the table set before them become a snare;
>   may it become retribution and a trap.
> May their eyes be darkened so that they cannot see,
>   and their backs be bent for ever.
> Pour out your wrath on them;
>   let your fierce anger overtake them.
> May their place be deserted;
>   let there be no one to dwell in their tents.

For they persecute those you wound
   and talk about the pain of those you hurt'

(Ps. 69:21-26).

Jonah showed the same violent reaction to his situation as David and proved the divine purpose even through his human anger, although Jonah, unlike David, did not actually utter an imprecation. It was not just the size of Nineveh or its blatant ungodliness which Jonah found abhorrent. It was the fact that Nineveh was the capital of Assyria, an enemy Gentile country, and that the God of the Jews was ordering him to go there. That stuck in Jonah's throat — in the boat, in the storm, in the fish but, above all, in repentant Nineveh. The disgruntled, if obedient, Jonah was still not a happy man. Then God spoke to Jonah a 'third' time — through the desert heat, the shelter of the plant, the withering of the plant and the sirocco blast, and finally, and most clearly, in words:

'But God said to Jonah, "Do you have a right to be angry about the vine?"

'"I do," he said. "I am angry enough to die."

'But the Lord said, "You have been concerned about this vine, though you did not tend it or make it grow. It sprang up overnight and died overnight. But Nineveh has more than a hundred and twenty thousand people who cannot tell their right hand from their left, and many cattle as well. Should I not be concerned about that great city?"'

(Jonah 4:9-11).

God taught Jonah of his love for all mankind, Gentile as well as Jew, and of his purpose to reach Gentile and Jew with the good news of salvation. God did this through Jonah's anger, his imprecations of judgement on godless, Gentile Nineveh. God makes the wrath of man to praise him, turns the curse into a blessing and perfects his purpose through the suffering of his angry servants.

A suffering Messiah

David's suffering in Psalm 69 is that of an innocent and godly man. It reflects also the human reaction of retribution towards enemies.

God used all three aspects to perfect his purposes in David's life. More than that, God uses all three aspects to prophesy the suffering of his Messiah, great David's greater Son, and to unlock the secret agonies of Jesus the Righteous Sufferer, God's one and only Son.

The New Testament presents the glory of the Messiah's work in his suffering and death. A triumphant Son of David as king and a sovereign Son of Man as judge were the popular dreams of Messiah. When Jesus came, however, the obscure, even discredited, image of a priestly, suffering Messiah came to the fore. In this, Isaiah's 'Suffering Servant' had pride of place, almost to the exclusion of other Old Testament prophecy. But there were other Old Testament pictures of Christ. The psalmist's 'Righteous Sufferer' complements Isaiah's 'Suffering Servant'. Prophets and Writings blend in a sorrowful picture of a suffering Messiah. Among the psalms, Psalm 69 is a perfect example. The innocence, godliness and retribution of David's pain are fulfilled in the sufferings of Jesus. The Servant who suffers is eminently righteous.

Christ our substitute

The *innocence* of David in relation to his trials finds fulfilment in Jesus' troubled life. The rationale behind Christ's persecution without a cause is explained on the principle of substitution. In this, Jesus himself is the great Teacher. Towards the end of his ministry, he attributed the bitterness of his enemies to the fulfilment of Scripture. He identified his lot with that of David in Psalm 69: 'But this is to fulfil what is written in their law: "They hated me without reason"' (John 15:25; cf. Ps. 69:4).

Jesus was conscious of the undeserved nature of his suffering because he endured the same great opposition as David did. David's persecutors were numerous, more than the hairs of his head. For Jesus, the range of enemies was even greater. It is not simply that the religious leaders of his day jealously took exception to his claims and drew off a fair proportion of the ordinary people to their side. That would be understandable. Nor is it that the early camp-followers, who appeared to support him, soon dwindled away and even turned against him when they realized his aims were spiritual in a non-political way. That was inevitable. It was rather that the world by its very nature hated him. His cause drew the venom of all men. There was a universal collusion against him and he had done nothing to deserve it.

Jesus' sense of his own innocence was increased as he perceived himself to be the victim of perverted justice. David complained that he was forced to pay back what he did not steal. He was treated like a thief when, in fact, he was a just man. A sense of injustice smouldered in his wounded heart. Jesus experienced the same. He had gone around doing good, healing the sick, cleansing lepers, exorcising the demon-possessed. He had even performed miracles as signs of his messiahhood. 'For which of these miracles do you stone me?' he had asked his enemies (John 10:32). They were treating him as the guilty party when, in fact, they themselves were guilty. If he had not performed miracles, they might have claimed to have had a clear conscience. But as it was, they had seen the miracles and still hated him. They were the guilty ones, not he. That increased his awareness of innocence and sense of injustice.

David suffered personally in the trauma of his persecution. Every bone of his body ached. Every organ of his senses was affected. Jesus suffered personally too. They hated him first and foremost. They persecuted him because of who and what he was. They treated him shamefully, the one who had done miracles among them. Jesus experienced the same aloneness, humanly speaking, as David had. Yet Jesus' grief plumbed even greater depths than David's. For not only was he suffering, but others were suffering because of him. Jesus' disciples were sharing in his persecution.

Jesus had taught his disciples earlier that he would suffer (Mark 8:31). He had not told them that they would suffer with him. Now he speaks plainly of this (John 13:19; 14:29; 15:27; 16:1-16). They would be put out of the synagogue, maligned, persecuted, even killed. People would do this to them supposedly in God's name. In a strange and intriguing way, the principle behind this action was substitution. The world hated the disciples because it hated Jesus first. If they persecuted Jesus, they would persecute his followers. If they obeyed his teaching, they would obey theirs. If they hated Christ's Father, they would hate Christ's friends. Just as Jesus had come from the Father to identify with sinful humanity, to substitute for his people in his death, to rid them of their sin and to unite them with himself and the Father, in order that they would belong no longer to the world but to God, so the world identifies Christ's followers with him, not with themselves. They are an alien race.

Christ's substitution affects his followers at every point. Christ's followers are privileged not only to believe in him, but to suffer with him.

This not only underlines Jesus' innocence in his suffering, it eases his pain. It provides grounds for an apparently groundless grief. It explains why 'They hated me without reason.' It provides rich comfort, too, for believers who suffer persecution for Christ's sake. It gives them a cause for the apparently causeless grief they endure, a reason for their undeserved suffering: 'If the world hates you, keep in mind that it hated me first. If you belonged to the world, it would love you as its own. As it is, you do not belong to the world, but I have chosen you out of the world. That is why the world hates you. Remember the words I spoke to you: "No servant is greater than his master." If they persecuted me, they will persecute you also. If they obeyed my teaching, they will obey yours also. They will treat you this way because of my name, for they do not know the One who sent me. If I had not come and spoken to them, they would not be guilty of sin. Now, however, they have no excuse for their sin. He who hates me hates my Father as well. If I had not done among them what no one else did, they would not be guilty of sin. But now they have seen these miracles, and yet they have hated both me and my Father. But this is to fulfil what is written in their Law: "They hated me without reason"' (John 15:18-25).

Sydney Carton, the hero of Charles Dickens' novel *A Tale of Two Cities*, is a telling human example of an innocent man suffering in place of another. The whole scene is one of misery and suffering — the violent days of the French Revolution, the endless tumbrils carrying the ill-fated aristocrats to their doom, the insatiable monster, *La Guillotine,* devouring its prey, the vengeful knitting ladies callously counting the victims.

Amid this is Sydney Carton, substituting for another even to death — the hurried change of clothing with Darnay, the success of his imposture, the agonizing last moments before his execution, the thoughts crowding his mind, his final words. All his undeserved suffering is made tolerable by his action of self-sacrifice. That eases the pain: 'I see the lives for which I lay down my life, peaceful, useful, prosperous and happy, in that England which I shall see no more... It is a far, far better thing that I do, than I have ever done; it is a far, far better rest that I go to than I have ever known.'

On an incomparably grander scale, this is the scene at Calvary —
the suffering of an innocent victim made meaningful through
substitution. As Jesus sees a world rampant in its hatred against
himself, as he contemplates the glaring injustice of his situation, as
he senses not only bitterness against his person but persecution of
his followers, he identifies with David in Psalm 69. The pain is
somewhat eased. The comfort to his disciples becomes pointedly
relevant. It is also through Christ's death pointedly precise and
definite, for it is substitutionary — not only in principle but in
practice as well. Just as Carton's death actually saved Darnay's life,
so Christ's substitutionary atonement actually saves God's elect,
chosen from eternity in Christ, the Lamb slain before earth's
foundation. Christ's death does not merely open up the possibility
of salvation, it saves his people from their sins. It is as definite as
that, for Christ's death is substitutionary.

David's undeserved grief in Psalm 69 is fulfilled in the suffering
and death of Jesus. Jesus explains this on the grounds of substitution.
Christ's substitution not only saves his people from their sin. At one
and the same time it causes them suffering and brings them comfort.
There is, after all, a cause behind their apparently causeless grief:
'They hated me without reason.'

Christ our sanctification

David's *godliness* in his suffering is fulfilled in Christ our sanctification. Here the motive behind the suffering is particularly clear.
Two New Testament writers stress the point. John, in his Gospel,
quoting from Psalm 69:9, recalls Christ's commitment to God: 'His
disciples remembered that it is written: "Zeal for your house will
consume me"' (John 2:17). Paul, in his letter to the Romans, quoting
from the same verse, cites Christ's selfless care for others amid his
own persecution: 'For even Christ did not please himself but, as it
is written: "The insults of those who insult you have fallen on me"'
(Rom. 15:3). Both quotations serve as a spur to Christians to find in
the righteous suffering of Christ a motive for sanctified living. Both
allusions, in quite a remarkable way, draw parallels between
David's godliness in trials and Christ's patient endurance.

John

The *context* of David's zeal for God in Psalm 69 is the enmity of others and his alienation from his own family. Indeed, David, deserted by friends and loved ones, finds refuge in God. The growing stressfulness of his lonely condition drives him on in his commitment to God.

John notes the same process in Jesus' life (John 2:12-25). At the outset of his ministry during the Passover, Jesus, living with his family and disciples at Capernaum, displayed zeal for God in clearing the temple of money-changers. It was then that his disciples remarked on their Master's commitment to God in terms of Psalm 69. Later, on the occasion of the Feast of Tabernacles, Jesus' brothers, who did not believe in him, urged him to go as a public figure to the feast and show his disciples his miracles. Jesus, however, visited the feast in his own time, and only on the final great day of the feast did he 'go public' in zeal for his Father's cause (John 7:1-37). Finally, at his death, when his own brothers appear to be absent, Jesus commends his mother to John's care. Jesus dies alone (John 19:26-27).

Other Gospel writers comment on the same process. Luke describes the rift between the twelve-year-old boy and his parents, as Jesus pursued his Father's business, asking questions of the teachers in the temple (Luke 2:41-52). Mark records how, on one occasion, Jesus' family regarded their son as 'out of his mind' (Mark 3:20-21). Jesus himself hints at this growing detachment from family and commitment to divine priority in his teaching. Who are his family? Those who follow him. What will this involve? Hating their nearest and dearest out of preferential love for God (Mark 3:31-35). Jesus, like David, experienced alienation from his family and loved ones amid the growing opposition of religious teachers and the ordinary people. This sense of isolation moves him in his commitment to God. Commitment to God's cause is not only reason but refuge in his lonely existence. Zeal for God's house is eating him up. In that, like David, Jesus finds both solace and purpose:

'After this he went down to Capernaum with his mother and brothers and his disciples. There they stayed for a few days.

'When it was almost time for the Jewish Passover, Jesus
went up to Jerusalem. In the temple courts he found men
selling cattle, sheep and doves, and others sitting at tables
exchanging money. So he made a whip out of cords, and
drove all from the temple area, both sheep and cattle; he scattered the coins of the money-changers and overturned their
tables. To those who sold doves he said, "Get these out of
here! How dare you turn my Father's house into a market!"'

'His disciples remembered that it is written, "Zeal for your
house will consume me"'

(John 2:12-17).

Paul

The *motive* behind David's zeal for God in Psalm 69 is a growing
awareness that he is suffering for God's sake. David is conscious
that he is a martyr for God. The reason for the violence and
opposition he experiences is simply that he is identifying with God's
cause and others are opposing him for this. 'The insults of those who
insult you fall on me,' David pleads with God (Ps. 69:9).

Paul picks up this same motive in Christ's life but traces out a
further implication. Opposition to Christ's ministry is not only a
spur to his commitment to God, but an incentive in his selfless care
for others. Paul sees Christ as so committed to God that his own self
becomes unimportant, as he spends himself in the service of others
for God's sake. In Christ, the two major thrusts of the law are
perfectly fulfilled. Christ loves God with all his heart and his
neighbour as himself.

In many ways Paul's perception of Christ here, like the background from which he writes, is unique. Paul, unlike John and the
disciples, did not have the opportunity of knowing Jesus personally.
He had met Jesus as one born 'at an abnormal time'. Yet his grasp
of the leading features of Christ's life is quite staggering. For Paul,
Christ, like David, was motivated through righteous suffering to
pursue God's will in caring for others amid the insensitive and bitter
opposition of the world around him.

The example Paul highlights from Christ's selfless attitude is
remarkable too. Drawing to the close of a letter in which he has presented the breathtaking blessings of Christ's death and resurrection,
Paul stresses the practical implications of Christ's life for Christian

living. Like Christ, Christians should have endless sympathy for those who are weak in the faith. Even when the issue might be clear to their own consciences, their concern for a weaker brother should take precedence. The reason for this is that Christ did not please himself but others, even those who insulted him. Christians should not please themselves but rather their neighbours for their good. Paul traces the motivation of this attitude in Christ back to Psalm 69:9: 'The insults of those who insult you fall on me.' The lines are clearly drawn.

Perhaps the most significant thing here is the way in which Paul teases out the principle of Scripture itself as a motivation not only for Christ but for the Christian as well. It is not simply that Psalm 69:9 represents a case in point where David's godly suffering is fulfilled in Christ's commitment to God and care for mankind. It is rather that *all Scripture* has behind it this purpose of stimulus and encouragement. All Scripture is fulfilled in Christ. We see this as we see Christ in the Psalms. But this is not all: the very influence which Scripture had on Jesus becomes for the believer, in principle, an incentive for daily Christian living especially in different circumstances. Paul illustrates the practical application of Scripture in general from the pointed case of Psalm 69:9 in particular. The Christ of the Psalms not only sets us an example but teaches us a lesson — the use of Scripture for the uplift of our own souls. In this, Paul's perception of Christ reaches its profoundest level.

All Paul says, and the way in which he says it, recalls David's motivation of godly suffering in Psalm 69 and he sees it fulfilled in Christ's commitment to God and selfless care for others: 'We who are strong ought to bear with the failings of the weak and not to please ourselves. Each of us should please his neighbour for his good, to build him up. For even Christ did not please himself but, as it is written: "The insults of those who insult you have fallen on me." For everything that was written in the past was written to teach us, so that through endurance and the encouragement of the Scriptures we might have hope' (Rom. 15:1-4).

Paul learns the lesson of Christ's commitment to God in a double way. Paul not only commends Christ's example to the Christians at Rome in terms of selfless care for others; he practises what he preaches. He discloses to believers at Corinth that Christ's commitment to God is the very motivation of his own missionary work as an apostle and he does so by quoting Psalm 69:13:

'As God's fellow-workers we urge you not to receive God's grace in vain. For he says,

"'In the time of my favour I heard you,
     and in the day of salvation I helped you."

'I tell you, now is the time of God's favour, now is the day of salvation'

(2 Cor. 6:1-2).

Paul has been opening his heart to the Christians at Corinth. It is Christ's love that compels him to do so. Convinced that one died for all, and therefore all died, those who live in Christ should no longer live for themselves but for him who died for them and was raised again (2 Cor. 5:14-15). That is the motivation of Paul and his friends in being 'Christ's ambassadors' and of their imploring Corinthians on Christ's behalf to be reconciled to God (2 Cor. 5:20).

The Corinthians, however, have not been open-hearted with Paul. They have been stilted in their response, withholding their affection from the apostolic band. They have done so in spite of the enormous hardships Paul has had to endure as Christ's ambassador. They have not been fair. They too must start opening wide their hearts (2 Cor. 6:3-13).

The specific aspect of selfless care for others which Christ's commitment to God induces in Paul is missionary zeal. Sanctification in this regard produces a passionate, unflagging earnestness to commend Christ to others, even at the expense of distressing hardships.

This is the path the Master trod
Should not the servant tread it still?

Missionary passion, hinted at in Psalm 2 and increasingly evident in Psalms 22 and 118, is implicit in the godliness of the righteous sufferer of Psalm 69. It is scorn endured 'for God's sake'. Christ our sanctification produces this selfless zeal in his children. It is a selfless care which longs to communicate the benefits of Christ and it often burns itself out in a consuming fire of passion.

The sad, short, yet glorious life of the missionary Henry Martyn recalls so well commitment to God and care for others amid a scene of godly suffering. I remember first reading the story of Martyn's life years ago and thinking to myself: 'Such a waste! Was he truly in God's will, pursuing his missionary endeavours to an early death, or was he misguided and misspent?' I have come to learn afresh the splendour of Henry Martyn's life.

Henry Martyn was brought up in Truro in Cornwall. He possessed a keen mind and his early days at Cambridge, though beset by initial problems, were soon to blossom into academic brilliance. His change of interest from mathematics to classics was a ready portent of the future. It was at Cambridge that he came to faith in Christ and this was to change the course of events dramatically. Under Charles Simeon's influence, Henry Martyn conceived a passion for missionary work in India. He was ultimately ordained to the Christian ministry and became a missionary candidate.

Martyn's home background was Christian but this added a sad twist to the tale of his life. His sister Sally, while delighted at his new-found faith in Christ, regarded her brother as unsuited for missionary work. More than this, Henry Martyn fell in love with a Christian girl, Lydia Grenfell, whom he loved dearly all his life but circumstances were such that they did not marry and he sacrificed this love for service to his Master.

Martyn's missionary work took him to India and eventually involved him in language and translation activity in the Middle East. Increasing ill health plagued him and, while planning to come home for Lydia to join him, he died still a relatively young man. R.T. France writes poignantly of his death: '"If He has a work for me to do", he had written in Shiraz, "I cannot die." But now the work was finished, and there, in an obscure corner of the Muslim world, the Armenian Christians buried an unknown English clergyman, "of whom the world was not worthy".'

Some words from Henry Martyn's diary unlock the secret zeal of his heart: 'I devoted myself unreservedly to the service of the Lord, to Him as to one who knew great conflict within, and my firm resolve, through His grace, of being His, though it should be with much tribulation.'

Henry Martyn, like David in Psalm 69 and Christ in his godly suffering, knew what it was to be consumed by a zeal for God and a selfless care for others. He also experienced the insults of those who insulted God falling on him. We should follow this pattern of sanctification in our own lives as believers.

Christ our Saviour

The element of *retribution* in David's suffering is fulfilled in
Christ's salvation. This is seen particularly in the way in which
salvation extends. The means by which Christ's kingdom spreads is
related to the theme of retribution.

Peter traces the unfolding purpose of salvation through Judas'
fate from Psalm 69:25:

> 'May his place be deserted;
>   let there be no one to dwell in it'
>
> (Acts 1:20).

Paul sees the plan of salvation in the inclusion of the Gentiles
through judgement on Israel from Psalm 69:22-23:

> 'May their table become a snare and a trap,
>   a stumbling-block and a retribution for them.
> May their eyes be darkened so they cannot see,
>   and their backs be bent for ever'
>
> (Rom. 11:9-10).

Both apostles claim that retribution in terms of God's judgement
is a means whereby Christ's salvation spreads and his kingdom
extends. Both see it as a fulfilment of David's anger. They are both
very conscious that God makes even the wrath of man to praise him.
Retribution works together in the divine purpose for the good of
man's salvation.

Peter

David's anger reaches its climax when he prays for destruction on
his enemies. He would see their camp deserted, their village a ghost-
town and consign their importance to oblivion, for they attribute his
sufferings to the judgement of God. They claim divine sanction for
their violent acts of persecution against him.

Peter recalls this at a critical time in the history of the early
church. Jesus had met with the apostles after his resurrection and
taught them about the kingdom of God. They were to wait in
Jerusalem until they received the promised gift of the Holy Spirit.

They wanted to know if Jesus would restore the kingdom to Israel in these days. He told them it was not for them to know God's timing. They must wait for power, for the Spirit. Then they would be witnesses in Jerusalem and to the ends of the earth. Soon after, Jesus ascended to heaven from Mount Olivet and they were left alone.

The disciples and the womenfolk waited and prayed, just as Jesus had told them. In those days, Peter sensed a directive from God through Scripture. It concerned the number of the apostles who would eventually bear witness to the kingdom throughout the world. The number was incomplete. It had been twelve, like the tribes of Israel. Now it was eleven. Judas was gone. David had prophesied this in his prayers of judgement in the psalms. Negatively speaking, he had foretold Judas' death in Psalm 69:25: 'May his place be deserted; let there be no one to dwell in it.' Positively, he had predicted Judas' replacement in Psalm 109:8: 'May another take his place of leadership.' They must appoint a replacement, one who had been with them from the beginning, who along with them would be a fellow-witness of Jesus' resurrection. They did so and eventually Matthias was chosen. Peter discerns God's purpose in salvation through the means of retribution in the fate of Judas.

Some have regarded this step as a mistake, the impulsive Peter dashing in where angels fear to tread. Had not Jesus commanded them simply to wait? There was nothing magical about the number twelve. The affirmation of Christ's resurrection did not depend on human testimony, complete or incomplete. Was Peter, as usual, forcing things, trying to bring about the restoration of the kingdom to Israel in his own time? Was it a classic example of Peter's lapsing from obedience? Was he carrying the infant church with him in his folly?

Was it really like that, however? The context of prayer, the compulsion of Scripture, the awareness that even during a 'holding period' the disciples must prepare themselves in every way possible, according to the available light of revelation, for the gift of the Spirit and for future kingdom work — these all suggest that Peter was right. It was not a lapse in obedience but a leading in faith. Peter discovers from Scripture the flow of God's purpose for Jesus' kingdom, even through the defection of Judas. Peter is convinced that God makes even the wrath of man the means of praising him and perceives it from the mouth of David in the fulfilment of Scripture, spoken by the Holy Spirit. Peter traces the purpose of salvation in

Judas' fate through David's retributive suffering. God turns the curse into a blessing. It is necessary for the replacement to be made in preparation for the coming power and the coming kingdom. They have no other option. Scripture requires it.

Paul

David's anger against his enemies reflects the hurt they have put him through: he is up to his neck in swirling waters; may their backs be crooked for ever. His throat is parched and his food poisoned; may their table be a snare to them. His eyes fail in looking for God; may their eyes be darkened so that they lose sight.

Paul picks up this last point as he reflects on God's saving plan to include Gentiles through judgement on Israel. Blind eyes, God's retributive punishment, are the link with David's experience. The link, however, is wider than simply with David. This theme of retributive judgement is in the Law and the Prophets as well as in the Psalms and Paul recalls it. Moses speaks of sightless eyes, deaf ears and lack of understanding at the time of the exodus from Egypt (Deut. 29:4). Isaiah mentions the same blind deaf stupor on Israel's part when God turned their captivity in Babylon (Isa. 29:10). The purpose behind this temporary exclusion of God's covenant people was that the Gentiles might be included, after which all Israel would be saved. The extension of salvation through retribution on his people was part of God's saving plan for both Jew and Gentile evident throughout the Old Testament.

'What then? What Israel sought so earnestly it did not obtain, but the elect did. The others were hardened, as it is written:

"'God gave them a spirit of stupor,
    eyes so that they could not see
    and ears so that they could not hear,
to this very day."

'And David says:

"'May their table become a snare and a trap,
    a stumbling-block and a retribution for them.

> May their eyes be darkened so they cannot see,
>   and their backs be bent for ever"'
>   (Rom. 11:7-9, quoting Deut. 29:4; Isa.29:10;
>   Ps. 69:22-23).

Many see Romans 9-11 as a digression from Paul's main theme in his letter. Their view is understandable. The sinful world, condemned before God, finding justification through Christ, the example of Abraham's faith, the blessings of access to grace, peace with God and new life in Christ reach a fitting climax in the unbreakable chain of predestinating glory at the close of chapter 8. The natural flow is to the commencement of sacrificial Christian living in practical sanctification from chapter 12 onwards. On this understanding, Paul's concern for Israel, chapters 9-11, is a personal intrusion jutting into his major theme.

This is not the case, however. The story of God's retributive judgement on Israel so that Gentiles might be saved is an integral part of the gospel. Branches broken off the natural olive-tree, Israel, so that unnatural branches, Gentiles, might be grafted in; Israel blinded, sightless under God's judgement, so that Gentiles might see and be saved — these are necessary steps in the plan of salvation. Paul clarifies this by writing in those chapters of God's sovereign choice, Israel's unbelief, the remnant of Israel and the Gentiles as engrafted branches. He proves from a host of Old Testament quotations, from all three sections of Scripture — Law, Prophets and Writings — that God's purpose is to save Gentile as well as Jew. The exciting thing about this purpose is its definite and precise nature. The purpose of God in the death of Christ is not simply to ingraft Gentiles generally into the people of God but to save a particular number of both Jews and Gentiles: 'What if God, choosing to show his wrath and make his power known, bore with great patience the objects of his wrath — prepared for destruction? What if he did this to make the riches of his glory known to the objects of his mercy, whom he prepared in advance for glory — even us, whom he also called, not only from the Jews but also from the Gentiles?' (Rom. 9:22-24). There is something incalculably definite about the plan of God in the death of Christ, a particular and definite atonement.

Paul specifically indicates that the means of this extension is the retributive judgement of God on his elect people. David's imprecations are part of a whole scriptural drift fulfilled in Christ's salvation. Jesus' enemies under judgement lead to the spread of his kingdom. God makes the wrath of man to praise him. Yet again, God turns curse into blessing.

A contrast between David and Christ

With regard to the whole aspect of retributive judgement, there is an interesting contrast between David and Christ. Obviously Christ did not mirror the statements of David. Under intense suffering, Christ showed great patience and understanding for his tormentors. He commanded love towards enemies and prayer for persecutors (Matt. 5:44). He called from the cross for the forgiveness of his execution-ers (Luke 23:34). David calls down curses on those who have mixed gall with his food and drink to poison him. May their table become a snare. Christ refuses the wine mixed with gall or myrrh given to those suffering crucifixion as an anaesthetic to deaden the pain. He will patiently bear the full fury of crucifixion, for he dies bearing sin as one cursed by God under judgement (Ps. 69:21; cf. Matt. 27:34; Mark 15:23).

Yet the idea of calling down judgment upon the enemies of God also finds a continuing thread in the New Testament. This might well be seen in the propitiatory aspects of Christ's death where the continuing anger of God against the wicked was directed against *Christ* in his substitutionary role.

In one sense, Christ was no longer the innocent of Psalm 69. Christ was the just, dying for the unjust; but he also became sin for us and, as such, legitimately could be punished for sin. Peter writes of Christ committing himself to the righteous Judge, as though God's continuing anger against the wicked persists alongside Christ's own example, in contrast to David's (1 Peter 2:23). The point, however, is that while David was innocent, Christ, as our substitute, was not. David's imprecatory prayer is a bold statement of the justice of God's wrath against transgressors. Christ's patient suffering means that he was the channel and the receptacle for the wrath of God against sin. God was making his wrath against the God-man himself to praise him.

Communism had been the great scourge of Christianity. We feared the undermining influence of this human philosophy so much that many regarded Communism as the Antichrist. Then it happened! God toppled the whole regime. In a short, sharp series of events this colossus, which bestrode the world like a mammoth beast, suddenly became powerless and virtually vanished. Miraculously, doors were opened that had been long and fast closed to the gospel. Border checkpoints ignored, no, welcomed Bibles! Churches, oppressed and depressed, began to emerge vitally and to show that God had not left himself without a witness and that there were many more than in the capitalist West brandishing gospel light. God had worked a miracle. He used the wrath of man to praise him. He turned the curse into a blessing. Retributive judgement served to honour and spread the gospel.

I read recently an interesting and exciting twist to the story. We could easily get the impression that Europe is ablaze with revival. Sadly, this is not the case yet. The Peloponnese is a vast mountainous area of southern Greece. It is virtually an island linked to the mainland through the bridges of the Corinthian canal. The Greek Orthodox Church predominates and hinders the gospel. But some strands of evangelical life persist. The Greek Evangelical Church and the Free Evangelical Church, once distant from each other, are now nearing in fellowship. In this somewhat depressing scenario, a pastor of the Free Evangelical Church in Corinth, when asked what believers at home should pray for, replied, 'Do not ask them to pray that we will stand up under persecution; do not ask them to pray that things will get easier for us. Ask them to pray that we will live lives which are holy and glorifying to God.'

David prayed for retribution on his enemies and God completed the story in the propitiatory death of Christ and in the outspread of the gospel of the kingdom. Jesus prayed for forgiveness for his foes. Successive generations of believers, like those in Communist lands and southern Greece, have sought to do the same. God answers those prayers. His retributive judgement serves his purpose, not only to fulfil the promise of Christ the Saviour, but to spread his kingdom of salvation to the ends of the earth.

David in Psalm 69 is a righteous sufferer. Innocence, godliness and retribution blend in his sorrowful lot. These themes find fulfilment in Christ the Righteous Sufferer. David's innocence is echoed in Christ our substitute, who leaves us an example that we should follow in his footsteps. David's godliness reaches its climax in Christ our sanctification, who calls for total commitment to God and selfless care for others. David's prayers of retribution are realized in the purpose and plan of Christ our Saviour. God still uses our anguished, oppressed circumstances to extend his work, makes the wrath of man to praise him, turns the curse into a blessing. David's 'Righteous Sufferer' perfectly complements Isaiah's 'Suffering Servant' in the person of our Lord Jesus Christ. Psalm 69 makes this abundantly clear. Jesus is the Righteous Sufferer.

4.
Dying Victim

Psalm 22 is 'not a description of illness but of an execution'. In that lies both its problem and its glory. It is difficult to identify the psalm with any particular incident in David's life. The frightening days of Saul's persecution or the frustrating times of Absalom's rebellion may well lie in the background. We can understand David's hardships to have been so intense that he depicts himself not just as a sick man, but as a condemned one.

That difficulty, however, points to the message of the psalm. While the details are roughly identifiable with David's experience, they point forward majestically to David's greater Son. Psalm 22 is, above all, prophecy. Unfulfilled in David's life, it finds realization in Christ's. But the story starts with David and there we must begin.

Anguish

The psalm opens on a scene of mental suffering. David is in dreadful turmoil for the worst of all reasons — he feels that God has deserted him. Criticism, opposition, even persecution is tolerable, but abandonment by God is an impossible plight. Contradiction lies at the heart of his dilemma. David affirms the might of God. He is EL, the strong God. David professes personal faith in this God. 'My God,' he cries. Yet this is his problem. He cries, but there is no answer. He looks, but there is no intervention. He believes, but there is no relief. The heavens are like brass. The situation remains unchanged. God is King enthroned in heaven; David is a worm tunnelling through

endless earth. The two are incompatible and irreconcilable. God is
not there. He has abandoned David. Yet is he not a strong God and
David's God? This glaring contradiction gnaws at the heart of
David's faith.

David's mental anguish is compounded by the treatment he
receives from the people. He is king over a nation whose tradition
had known constant deliverance by Jehovah. Lines of generations
trusted in the covenant God and he rescued them. Now, it is as
though he, David, was to blame for this abandonment. The people
insult not only David, but his faith and his God. That is the last straw.
How alone mentally could a man be?

> 'My God, my God, why have you forsaken me?
>> Why are you so far from saving me,
>> so far from the words of my groaning?
> O my God, I cry out by day, but you do not answer,
>> by night, and am not silent.
> Yet you are enthroned as the Holy One;
>> you are the praise of Israel.
> In you our fathers put their trust;
>> they trusted and you delivered them.
> They cried to you and were saved;
>> in you they trusted and were not disappointed.
> But I am a worm and not a man,
>> scorned by men and despised by the people.
> All who see me mock me;
>> they hurl insults, shaking their heads:
> "He trusts in the Lord;
>> let the Lord rescue him.
> Let him deliver him,
>> since he delights in him"'

(Ps. 22:1-8).

Pain

Physical suffering is part of David's lot too. He is under attack in the
wasteland from a host of wild animals, all equally ferocious and
angry for prey. Bulls, lions, packs of jackals and wild oxen prowl

around as he seeks security away from human enemies. He is naturally fearful. Not a cowardly man by disposition — he tackled a lion and a bear when tending sheep — he finds his resources of strength are drained. He is poured out like water. His heart melts like wax. His strength is brittle like dry pottery. He fears the infliction of further pain. He thinks of his poor, weak, tired body — his tongue sticking to his mouth; his hands and feet gashed with cuts; his bones, every one of them aching, pushing through his ribcage; his clothes, such as they are, tattered and torn — the only miserable possessions of a miserable man, over which those vengeful enemies one day will gloat, if and when they find him. His body has had enough. Mental anguish tortures him. Physical pain nauseates him. He pleads with God, his strength, to deliver him:

> 'Many bulls surround me;
>> strong bulls of Bashan encircle me.
> Roaring lions tearing their prey
>> open their mouths wide against me.
> I am poured out like water,
>> and all my bones are out of joint.
> My heart has turned to wax;
>> it has melted away within me.
> My strength is dried up like a potsherd,
>> and my tongue sticks to the roof of my mouth;
>> you lay me in the dust of death.
> Dogs have surrounded me;
>> a band of evil men has encircled me,
>> they have pierced my hands and my feet.
> I can count all my bones;
>> people stare and gloat over me.
> They divide my garments among them
>> and cast lots for my clothing.
> But you, O Lord, be not far off;
>> O my Strength, come quickly to help me.
> Deliver my life from the sword,
>> my precious life from the power of the dogs.
> Rescue me from the mouth of the lions;
>> save me from the horns of the wild oxen'
>
>> (Ps. 22:12-21).

Triumph

The mood suddenly changes. Obviously deliverance has come. God has intervened. David now sings praise to God before the great assembly. The theme of his song is God himself, who is no longer distant but now a very present help in time of trouble. David prepares a feast to celebrate, a thank-offering. That particular sacrifice presented the opportunity not only to affirm God's greatness, but to enjoy a fellowship meal with God's people. That is the wonderful thing about Jehovah's deliverance. It not only restores relationships with himself but with his people as well. David declares God's virtues to his covenant brothers who were recently among his bitterest enemies. The poor commoners of Jerusalem also share in the celebrations. They eat their full and are satisfied, listening to their king as he recites his vows to God.

The victory song spreads further afield. Gentiles are drawn to faith in Israel's God. All the ends of the earth remember and trust in the Lord — rich and poor, present generations and future posterity. There is no limit to the extension of Jehovah's kingdom, for dominion belongs to the Lord. David concludes with the simple but glorious reason for this: 'for he has done it'. God has answered David's prayer. God has finished his saving work — to perfection.

> 'I will declare your name to my brothers;
>   in the congregation I will praise you.
> You who fear the Lord, praise him!
>   All you descendants of Jacob, honour him!
> Revere him, all you descendants of Israel!
> For he has not despised or disdained
>   the suffering of the afflicted one;
> he has not hidden his face from him
>   but has listened to his cry for help.
> From you comes the theme of my praise in the great
>   assembly;
>   before those who fear you will I fulfil my vows.
> The poor will eat and be satisfied;
>   they who seek the Lord will praise him —
>   may your hearts live for ever!
> All the ends of the earth
>   will remember and turn to the Lord,

and all the families of the nations
    will bow down before him,
for dominion belongs to the Lord
    and he rules over the nations.
All the rich of the earth will feast and worship;
    all who go down to the dust will kneel before him —
    those who cannot keep themselves alive.
Posterity will serve him;
    future generations will be told about the Lord.
They will proclaim his righteousness
    to a people yet unborn—
    for he has done it'

(Ps. 22:22-31).

Crucifixion

Psalm 22 will always be associated with Christ's death if, for no other reason than that Jesus quoted its opening words on the cross. Some suggest that Jesus quoted the entire psalm and, then, when he cried in triumph, 'Finished!' he echoed the closing thought of the psalmist: 'for he has done it' (Ps. 22:31). Others go further. They claim that Jesus, on the cross, even in his parched condition, began by recalling Psalm 22 and then continued quoting from the psalter: the Shepherd's care of Psalm 23; Jehovah's kingship of Psalm 24; the plaintiff's plea of Psalms 25 and 26; the Lord as a light and a rock in Psalms 27 and 28; the power of God's Word and salvation in Psalms 29 and 30 — all climaxed in the final commitment: 'Father, into your hands I commit my spirit' (Luke 23:46; cf. Ps. 31:5).

Whether this was so or not, the detailed and exact fulfilment of so many features of Psalm 22 in the death of Christ is staggering. Crucifixion lies at the heart of this fulfilment. It was a horrible form of execution. Derek Thomas explains this in vivid terms: 'Crucifixion is thought to have been an invention of the Persians, who worshipped a god of the ground called Ormayed. So as not to defile the ground, executions were performed by lifting the victims into the air. Alexander the Great introduced the practice into Egypt and Carthage. The Romans are thought to have copied it from the Carthaginians.

'Flavius Josephus, the famous Jewish historian and an adviser to Titus during the siege of Jerusalem, had observed many crucifixions and called them "the most wretched deaths". Hardened Roman soldiers often felt pity for their victims. The process was excruciatingly awful. Swelling wounds, congealing blood and raging fever combined to make crucifixion a painful ordeal. For six hours, from 9.00 to 3.00, Jesus endured it.'

The mockery, the thirst, the piercing of hands and feet, the nakedness and dispersal of clothing all inevitably hark back to Psalm 22. The mental and physical suffering of Jesus is retold against this specific background. Not just Christ's words, but the whole scenario of Golgotha recalls this psalm, and does so penetratingly and intentionally. The details of Psalm 22 which remain unfulfilled in David's experience find clear fulfilment in Jesus' death. This is why the psalm is not a description of illness, but of execution. Indeed, the detailed, exact fulfilment of Psalm 22 in Jesus' death presents Calvary as the precise answer to man's condemned plight in sin.

Dereliction

David suffered dereliction as he felt deserted by God and despised by the people. Jesus suffered similar mental anguish as he hung on the cross. The horror of Jesus' plight, however, becomes fearful when we compare his situation with that of David.

Separation

The sense of inner contradiction David experienced is magnified beyond all comprehension in Jesus' case. David's awareness of God's caring presence had been from early on: the troubled days of Saul's vengeance, the tense times of Absalom's rebellion. Jesus' consciousness predates this. Before time, he had known a oneness with God, a sharing of eternal glory, an enjoyment of purposeful oneness clouded only now, in part, by the veil of flesh. To conceive of total rupture of such a relationship would be unthinkable for Jesus. It was alien to his total self-nature, to very existence as he knew it. David was a servant of God as king. However close this bond, however grave the sense of obligation, it pales into insignificance beside Jesus' experience of abandonment. For he is Son, not servant, of the very nature and essence of his Father God. Jesus' cry, 'My God, my God, why have you forsaken me?' expresses the ultimate in dereliction. It is the cry of an eternal Son orphaned from his eternal Father, a oneness of nature split in fragmented torture and loneliness.

Yet every syllable of Jesus' cry of separation from his Father earned for his people an eternal unity with God. He called out unanswered to his Father God, the Strong One, so that the ring of response might sound in our hearts as we are effectively called by the strength of the same mighty God. He questioned his abandonment, not in faithless rebellion but in quiet resignation, so that we might discover the answer in God's justifying grace: total and final acquittal of our guilt, peace of conscience with God for ever. He was God's orphaned Son so that we might be eternally adopted into God's family. Each strain of his agonized cry finds its answer in redeeming grace — called, justified, adopted. His separation from God promises our unity with God.

Scorn

His scornful treatment by men wins us God's favour. How despised Christ was! David knew the loneliness of scorn in his experience — the enmity against his leadership, the criticism of advisers, the hurled insults of followers, the shaking heads, the slur on his faith in God. Those features are particularly pointed up in the story of Christ's sufferings — the wagging heads, the pursed lips, the words of insult maligning his faith. But for Christ the scorn assumes proportions of enormity. David made mistakes and was justly judged by his subjects. Christ did only good, for in him was no sin, and yet he earned the enmity of a whole world against him. Christ knew the insults against David repeated against himself when he pleaded in David's words for God's help. He experienced the endless kicking of a victim when he was down, the quoting by others against him of the very Scriptures he himself had used. 'Those who passed by hurled insults at him, shaking their heads... "He trusts in God. Let God rescue him now if he wants him, for he said, 'I am the Son of God'"' (Matt. 27:39,43; cf Ps. 22:7-8).

Yet the scorn poured on him wins us God's favour. Christ endures the hatred of men so that we might know the love of God.

He does this as our substitute, bearing our sins in his body on the tree. The punishment which brought about our peace was laid on him. The raucous mockery and ribald insults of soldiers and people become, through Christ's suffering, the sweet tones of God's forgiveness. The fulfilment of Psalm 22 at Golgotha makes this clear. For separation we gain unity; for scorn, favour. Christ's death becomes the precise answer to our need.

Mental anguish distorts relationships. I learned that through a friend's experience. She had come to faith through disturbed circumstances and, some years later, had had a nervous breakdown. My heart bled for her as she explained her state of mind to me. The old paranoia of fear returned. She found crowds distasteful; people, she thought, were talking about her, ganging up against her. Worst of all, she felt God had left her. Her Bible readings were meaningless; her mind was obsessed with the question 'Why?' Why had God abandoned her, left her like this, so dreadfully confused and alone? Was God really there at all? Was there a God at all?

We prayed earnestly both with her and for her. God healed her and the distortion disappeared. People were there to help her. Scripture again became meaningful. God was not dead but very much alive, faith no longer a delusion but a gripping reality. Through his abandonment on the cross, Jesus had healed her. His separation brought her back to God. Of course, my friend had been a Christian before her illness and in healing her of her breakdown, God had also restored her spiritually. The psychological and spiritual must be kept distinct. But what had happened to my Christian friend psychologically, happens to all men spiritually. Sin distorts and separates, scorns and insults us, cuts us off from God and alienates us from men. Jesus, by his mental anguish on Calvary, answers that problem. Through his tortured abandonment, we can find peace with God. Relationships need no longer remain broken and distorted but can be gloriously restored.

> Throned upon the awful tree,
> King of grief, I watch with thee.
> Darkness veils thine anguished face:
> None its lines of woe can trace:
> None can tell what pangs unknown
> Hold thee silent and alone—

Silent through those three dread hours,
Wrestling with the evil powers,
Left alone with human sin,
Gloom around thee and within,
Till the appointed time is nigh,
Till the Lamb of God may die.

Hark, that cry that peals aloud
Upward through the whelming cloud!
Thou, the Father's only Son,
Thou, his own Anointed One,
Thou dost ask him — can it be?—
'Why hast thou forsaken me?'

Lord, should fear and anguish roll
Darkly o'er my sinful soul,
Thou, who once wast thus bereft
That thine own might ne'er be left,
Teach me by that bitter cry
In the gloom to know thee nigh.

(John Ellerton)

Distress

For David, emotional suffering was combined with physical. Pain of body accompanied anguish of spirit. This was also fulfilled in Christ's experience. Again the fulfilment is vivid, as though the Gospel writers had this psalm in mind as they told the lurid details. Again the sense of contrast is impressive. What David describes merely previews the horror of Christ's experience. The reality far transcends the prediction. Again precise results are implied. Christ's distress earns our relief. His pains of death produce our spiritual life. By his wounds we are healed.

Thirst

Thirst figures prominently in the psalmist's distress:

'My strength is dried up like a potsherd,
    and my tongue sticks to the roof of my mouth'
                                        (Ps. 22:15).

David obviously knew many occasions of physical thirst. None
is more poignantly described than that towards the end of his life
when he longs for a drink from the well near the gate at Bethlehem.
In the event, though thirsty from battle, David will not drink this
dearly earned water, gained through his warriors' courage, but pours
it out before the Lord.

The theme of thirst threads through the crucifixion story. Often
criminals, when being nailed to the cross, would be offered wine
mixed with myrrh to drink, as an anaesthetic to dull the pain. This
offer is made to Jesus but he pointedly refuses. As he vowed in
Gethsemane, he will drink the cup of anguish to its bitter dregs. He
will take nothing to offset the fury of his God-appointed suffering.
He will endure the fierceness of his punishment consciously.

Later, on the cross, to fulfil Scripture, Jesus cries, 'I thirst.' A
soldier holds to his lips a sponge dipped in sour wine on the end of
a hyssop reed and he drinks. Jesus' earlier refusal and later acceptance of the wine fulfils, in a telling way, Psalm 22:15. It also shows
the difference between the thirst of David and that of Christ.
David's refusal was a denial of personal satisfaction; Christ's
refusal was a submission to the full consciousness of the fury of
judgement. Christ's acceptance, after the endurance of his suffering,
enabled him to cry in victory, 'Finished!' The very pattern of
Christ's thirst fulfils the scope of Psalm 22.

His are the thousand sparkling rills
That from a thousand fountains burst,
And fill with music all the hills;
And yet he saith, 'I thirst.'

But more than pains that racked him then
Was the deep longing thirst divine
That thirsted for the souls of men;
Dear Lord, and one was mine!
                                        (Cecil Frances Alexander)

Jesus endured human thirst that we might know eternal satisfaction. He had already explained those details to a lone Samaritan woman. If she drank of the water that he gave her, she would never thirst again (John 4:13-14). Later, he told Jewish teachers that, unless they ate the flesh and drank the blood of the Son of Man, they would have no life in them (John 6:53). On Calvary, Christ practised fatefully what he had earlier preached. He thirsted to death that we might be satisfied with life.

Wounding

Wounds inflicted on the psalmist were part of the pain he suffered. Again, the description is vivid:

> 'Dogs have surrounded me;
>   a band of evil men has encircled me,
>   they have pierced my hands and my feet'
>
> (Ps. 22:16).

C. H. Spurgeon notes the forward thrust of this reference. 'This can by no means refer to David, or to anyone but Jesus of Nazareth, the once crucified but now exalted Son of God. Pause, dear reader, and view the wounds of thy Redeemer.' Spurgeon is right and yet David here, even in prophecy, reflects out of his own experience. The physical pain he endures from his human enemies resembles bites on his hands and feet by vicious desert dogs or ravenous lions.

The intensity of this pain is enlarged when our gaze moves from David in the desert to Jesus on the cross. The focus of that gaze is fixed as we consider how exactly the description of Psalm 22:16, the piercing of hands and feet, fits Calvary. The evangelists summarize it in one horrid word: 'Crucified'. In a short, terse statement they all mark the end of their Master's ministry, for crucifixion involved the piercing of hands and feet: 'And they crucified him' (Mark 15:24; cf. Matt. 27:35; Luke 23:33; John 19:18).

John Stevenson brings home the physical horror of this: 'Of all sanguinary punishments, that of crucifixion is one of the most dreadful—no vital part is immediately affected by it. The hands and feet which are furnished with the most numerous and sensitive organs are perforated with nails, which must necessarily be of some size to suit their intended purpose. The tearing asunder of the tender fibres of the hands and feet, the lacerating of so many nerves, and bursting of so many blood vessels, must be productive of intense agony. The nerves of the hand and foot are intimately connected through the arm and leg with the nerves of the whole body; their laceration therefore must be felt over the entire frame ... when, therefore, the hands and feet of our blessed Lord were transfixed with nails he must have felt the sharpest pangs shoot through every part of his body. Supported only by his lacerated limbs, and suspended from his pierced hands, our Lord had nearly six hours of torment to endure.'

It is strange how the picture of those wounds linger on in Scripture, a continuing testimony to Christ's dying sorrow: 'Unless I see the nail marks in his hands and put my finger where the nails were, and put my hand into his side, I will not believe it,' vowed Thomas (John 20:25). 'Put your finger here; see my hands. Reach out your hand and put it into my side. Stop doubting and believe,' responded Jesus (John 20:27). 'Finally, let no one cause me trouble, for I bear on my body the marks of Jesus,' wrote Paul (Gal. 6:17). What Isaiah foretold of Zion being engraved on the palms of God's hands, what Zechariah predicted of God's people viewing the one whom they had pierced, David prophesies of the piercing of the Messiah's hands and feet. John sees this in part fulfilled at Calvary: 'As another scripture says, "They will look on the one they have pierced"' (John 19:37; cf Zech. 12:10). John sees its ultimate fulfilment at Jesus' return:

> 'Look, he is coming with clouds,
>   and every eye will see him,
> even those who pierced him;
>   and all the peoples of the earth will mourn because of him.
>   So shall it be! Amen'
>   (Rev. 1:7).

Christ's pierced hands and feet are not just a continuing witness to his suffering but a clarion call to healing. Just as the punishment that brought us peace was laid on him, so by his wounds we are healed. His thirst brings us satisfaction, his wounds provide healing. All his pain and agony tend to that glorious end.

Nakedness

The shame of nakedness and the indignity of dispossessed clothing were also the psalmist's lot in suffering:

'They divide my garments among them
   and cast lots for my clothing'

(Ps. 22:18).

But where do we find this in David's experience? True, in general, David may often have watched his own troops share out among themselves the booty and spoils of victory. In particular, he may have remembered, in the early days, how ashamed his wife Michal felt of him, as he danced in triumph naked before the Lord. He may even have reflected on days when his clothing was worn and torn as he lay in the cave of Adullam or in the hillside near Saul's encampment. That was a chilling memory, as he sat enthroned in Jerusalem and pulled his royal robes closely about him. But this statement does not fit exactly anything in David's lifetime.

For Jesus, however, it fits precisely. The whole ignominy of nakedness and bartered clothing is woven into the crucifixion story as forcefully as the theme of pierced hands and feet. The soldiers stripped Jesus to flog him. They clothed him in purple to crown and mock him. They stripped him again to crucify him. They diced for his garments at the foot of the cross.

We picture Jesus modestly hanging in agony, a loincloth about his waist. The truth may have been very different. He was probably stark naked. J. P. Lange says, 'Perfectly naked did the *cruciarii* hang upon the cross, and the executioners received their clothes. There is nothing to show that there was a cloth even round the loins. The clothes became the property of the soldiers, after Roman usage. The outer garment was divided probably into four, by ripping up the seams. Four soldiers were counted off as a guard by the Roman code. The undergarment could not be divided being woven, and this led the soldiers to dice-throwing.'

Matthew, Mark and Luke boldly note the dispersion of clothes as part of the crucifixion. No other comment is necessary. The allusion to Psalm 22 is perfectly clear. John explains the precise detail of difference: the outer garments given to each of the four soldiers, the

seamless tunic falling to the dice. John claims this in fulfilment of
Scripture, quoting Psalm 22:18. That was why the soldiers did
exactly what they did, he adds. The shame of his naked body on the
cross above, the ignominy of his only possessions bartered below —
all constituted an unforgettable fulfilment of the psalmist's prophecy. How low did the Son of God stoop! In what shame and
degradation did the Son of Man suffer! What painful distress lingers
on in this shameful sight of a naked and neglected Lord!

Yet his nakedness provides us with clothing; his neglect brings
us care; his shame clothes us with glory. To that end he lived; for that
purpose he died. Our first parents fell in sin and felt the shame of
nakedness. God made garments for them to cover their shame. The
Son of Man came and taught, in his state of humiliation, the
necessity of his provision of a wedding garment. Otherwise, we are
barred from the feast (Matt. 22:11-14). The Son of God, in his state
of exaltation, called to the church at Laodicea in the same vein: 'You
say, "I am rich; I have acquired wealth and do not need a thing." But
you do not realize that you are wretched, pitiful, poor, blind and
naked. I counsel you to buy from me gold refined in the fire, so that
you can become rich; and white clothes to wear, so that you can
cover your shameful nakedness; and salve to put on your eyes, so
that you can see' (Rev. 3:17-18).

The exalted Lord will one day ride in glory dressed in a robe
dipped in blood, his armies following him dressed in fine linen,
white and clean, riding on white horses (Rev. 19:11-16). What a day
that will be, the shame of his nakedness vindicated, the ignominy of
his dispossession justified, the defeat of his cross becoming his
people's song of triumph! It will have been all gloriously worth-
while — the nakedness, the shame, the distress.

Jesus, thy blood and righteousness
My beauty are, my glorious dress;
'Midst flaming worlds, in these arrayed
With joy shall I lift up my head.

Bold shall I stand in thy great day;
For who aught to my charge shall lay?
Fully absolved through these I am
From sin and fear, from guilt and shame.
                                               (Nicolaus von Zinzendorf).

Jean had approached me on a number of occasions about becoming a Christian. Eventually, it came to the point where she came to faith in Christ. We spoke often in those days. She asked me to explain some details of Scripture to her, started coming to the midweek meeting, showed signs of growth in grace. Then it seemed to stop. She assured me her health was not too good. Later came the mastectomy; two years afterwards terminal liver cancer.

I watched Jean suffer — the mental anguish of bad news, the physical pain of approaching death. I saw her thirst, her poor tongue covered in thrush with the side-effects of medication, as I and the family helped her drink through a straw. I looked at her in pain, the wounds of bodily discomfort eased by the continual dosage of morphine. I felt the indignity of her state, the massive weakness like a great shame covering her once bright and active life. It brought Calvary back to me — the thirst, the wounds, the nakedness.

Yet, in all her distress, Jean proved her faith. When the bad news first came, she told me that she was ready for whatever God wanted. She continued to hold on to snippets of Scripture as I read and prayed with her. On the flyleaf of her Bible she had written in her own hand two items of praise. One was the metrical version of Psalm 40, 'I waited for the Lord my God and patiently did bear,' over which she had noted, 'I love this hymn.' The other was 'What a friend we have in Jesus'. Over the words, 'Are we weak and heavy laden?', she had written and underlined the word, 'true'. Later, her husband showed me a doctrinal book on the Christian life she had been reading. As I preached on the day of her funeral I kept thinking of the words of the old minister: 'I found her in a state of nature, I led her to a state of grace, I left her in a state of glory.'

What a lot I learned as a pastor from Jean's experience! I saw a satisfaction amid human thirst, a healing beyond physical wounds, a dignity covering the nakedness of suffering. I saw the benefits of the Redeemer's death transferred with deliberation and precision to a believer's life, as she moved from grace to glory: satisfaction for thirst, healing for wounds, covering for nakedness. It was an experience I shall never forget.

Substitution

The graphic fulfilment of Psalm 22 in the portrayal of Jesus' death in the Gospels teaches the truth of Christ's vicarious substitutionary atonement, that is, that Jesus died in the place of the sinner, bearing his sin and his deserved punishment and that, in direct relation to that substitution, the repentant sinner gains eternal life. Christ's death brings to us eternal life: calling, justification, adoption, satisfaction, healing, covering, all through vicarious, substitutionary atonement.

Some have drawn back from the idea of substitution. They maintain it is too crude, a sacrificial aspect unworthy of New Testament teaching about the death of Christ. They prefer to see Christ as our representative in his suffering and death rather than our substitute. The death of Christ is indeed presented in this representative capacity — Christ died as our covenant head, the second Adam. But the New Testament goes beyond this and explains this representation in terms of substitution. Christ came not to be served but to serve, and to give his life a ransom for many (Mark 10:45). Christ gave himself as a ransom for all men (1 Tim. 2:6). Christ redeemed us from the curse of the law by becoming a curse for us (Gal. 3:13). Christ himself bore our sins in his body on the tree, so that we might die to sins and live for righteousness; by his wounds we have been healed (1 Peter 2:24).

Substitution is not simply one aspect of Christ's atonement. It is specifically through substitution that the benefits of Christ's death come to his people. His wounds provide healing. His righteousness, in the place of our unrighteousness, brings us to God. His sin-bearing means that his people die to sin and live for righteousness. Christ's substitution blesses his people with justification and motivates them to sanctification. It is not simply that Christ died and rose again and, in a symbolic way, we somehow are forgiven and made ready for heaven. Christ died and rose again in our place so that we might die to sin and live to righteousness.

James Denney, in his classic work *The Death of Christ*, commenting on 1 Peter 2:24, expresses this finely: 'Once we understand what Christ's death means — once we receive the apostolic testimony that in that death He was taking all our responsibilities upon Him — no explanation may be needed. The love which is the motive of it acts immediately upon the sinful; gratitude exerts an irresistible constraint. His responsibility means our emancipation; His death our life; His bleeding wound our healing. Whoever says "He bore our sins" says substitution; and to say substitution is to say something which involves an immeasurable obligation to Christ, and has therefore in it incalculable motive power. This is the answer to some of the objections which are commonly made to the idea of substitution on moral grounds. They fail to take account of the sinner's sense of debt to Christ for what He has done, a sense of debt which it is not too much to designate as the most intimate, intense and uniform characteristic of New Testament life. It is this which bars out all ideas of being saved from the consequences of sin, while living on in sin itself. It is so profound that the whole being of the Christian is changed by it. It is so strong that it extinguishes and creates at the one time. Under the impression of it, to use the apostle's words here, the aim of Christ's bearing of our sins is fulfilled in us — we die to the sins and live to righteousness.'

The substitutionary atonement of the dying victim brings us to the very heart of the gospel. It is not an isolated facet but an integral part. It is not an optional extra but of the very essence of a whole scheme of salvation revealed to us in Scripture. Calvary in terms of substitution, and substitution of a most definite and particular nature, for the elect of God, is the strength and glory of the gospel.

C. H. Spurgeon was so right when he declared: 'I have my own private opinion that there is no such thing as preaching Christ and Him crucified, unless we preach what is nowadays called Calvinism. It is a nickname to call it Calvinism; Calvinism is the gospel, and nothing else. I do not believe we can preach the gospel ... unless we preach the sovereignty of God in His dispensation of grace; nor unless we exalt the electing, unchangeable, eternal, immutable, conquering love of Jehovah; nor do I think we can preach the gospel unless we base it upon the special and particular redemption of His elect and chosen people which Christ wrought out upon the Cross; nor can I comprehend a gospel which lets saints fall away after they are called.'

Dominion

The final section of the psalm stands in stark contrast with the earlier part. The anguish and pain are past and triumph is in the air. Dereliction and distress give way to dominion on all sides. It is victory after suffering — indeed, victory through suffering. The torment of David's pain is inextricably linked with the joy of triumph. The former not only leads to the latter; it causes it. David's prayer in trouble produces his praise of victory in deliverance. It is victory through suffering.

Identification

The remarkable thing is that there is only one New Testament quotation from this final section of Psalm 22. The earlier part is quoted a number of times and the details are precisely linked with the crucifixion. The one passage that is quoted is verse 22 and, while referring to Christ's death, the New Testament writer essentially stresses Christ's incarnation in connection with his death:

> 'In bringing many sons to glory, it was fitting that God, for whom and through whom everything exists, should make the author of their salvation perfect through suffering. Both the one who makes men holy and those who are made holy are of the same family. So Jesus is not ashamed to call them brothers. He says,

> > "'I will declare your name to my brothers;
> > in the presence of the congregation I will sing your praises"'

> > > (Heb. 2:10-12; cf. Ps. 22:22).

David is glad to declare God's name to his brothers. He is unashamed of the deliverance God has given him. Indeed, he exults publicly in it. Perhaps some of those 'brothers' had been David's critics, blaming him for misgovernment, ostracizing him in his difficulties. David forgives and forgets all that. God has heard and has answered his cry for help. That is all that matters. Now he identifies with his brothers in triumph.

Christ's identification far transcends this. By nature, David was one with his brothers in humanity, race and professed religion. Christ was very different. He voluntarily took upon himself humanity in order to identify with and, ultimately, to deliver those whom he would eventually call brothers. Christ's was a self-enforced, a self-assumed, a condescending identification. It involved sacrificing the intimacy of communion with God his Father, divesting himself, in part, of his royal regalia and taking on himself the form of a creature. For David, it was a matter of swallowing his pride and past insults. For Christ, it was a case of assuming an alien nature and dying a felon's death. At that level, the two are incomparable. That is why the writer to the Hebrews notes Christ's lack of shame in calling his people brothers. In fact, it involved great shame and glaring indignity all along the line.

Expansion

The triumph of dominion involved not only identification but also expansion. There is no direct quotation to this effect, but it is an implication of verse 22 as it is quoted in Hebrews. The extension of dominion to the Gentiles through sufferings and death further convinces Calvin of the prophetic nature of Psalm 22. Of verse 22 he writes, 'I have already repeatedly stated (and it is also easy to prove it from the end of this psalm), that under the figure of David, Christ has been here shadowed forth to us.' Of verse 27 he claims, '"All the ends of the earth shall remember." This passage, beyond all doubt, shows that David stops not at his own person but that under himself, as a type, he describes the promised Messiah.'

David had received the covenant promise of God that his dynastic line would be preserved. But this related only to God's ancient covenant people. In Psalm 22 David speaks of a situation where all the ends of the earth will remember and turn to the Lord, where all the families of nations will bow down before him, where even future generations will share in this knowledge (Ps. 22:27,28,30,31). This is much more than the national expansion of Judah into a world power. This is a promise of spiritual dominion. What Abraham was promised about all families of the earth being blessed through himself, what Isaiah predicted of an endless Davidic kingdom which would include even Gentiles, what stubborn Jonah learnt about Assyrian Ninevites becoming the recipients of God's love, David here forecasts of the Messiah.

How perfectly this expansion was fulfilled through the sufferings and death of Christ! This, in large measure, is the theme of the book of Acts. Jesus had promised that his followers would be witnesses in Jerusalem, Judaea, Samaria and to the ends of the earth. Chapter by chapter, Luke's history unfolds this. From Jerusalem to Rome, Paul continually turns from unresponsive Jews to evangelize Gentiles. The story ends at Rome in that way (Acts 28:23-31). John reminds us of the ultimate victory, where, from every tribe and nation, past, present and future, there will be gathered a glorious church, triumphant before her Lord (Rev. 5:9-10). Psalm 22 forecasts all of this as a result of the Messiah's sufferings and death.

Completion

The psalm ends on a final note of triumph. God's dominion is complete. David unreservedly attributes this to God's great saving action:

> 'Posterity will serve him;
>   future generations will be told about the Lord.
> They will proclaim his righteousness
>   to a people yet unborn—
>   for he has done it'

> > > > > > (Ps. 22:30-31).

'For he has done it.' As a psalm of praise, the effectiveness of this dominion is due to God's saving action. As a prophecy of Messiah, it is fulfilled in Christ's triumphant claim on the cross: 'Finished!' This was uttered, not in pathetic distress, but in final dominion.

C. H. Spurgeon comments: 'Fathers shall teach their sons, who shall hand it down to their children; the burden of the story always being "that he hath done this", or, that "It is finished". Salvation's glorious work is done, there is peace on earth and glory in the highest. "It is finished"; these were the expiring words of the Lord Jesus, as they are the last words of this Psalm. May we by living faith be enabled to see our salvation finished by the death of Jesus!'

> 'Tis finish'd, 'Tis finish'd — was his latest voice;
> These sacred accents o'er,
> He bow'd his head, gave up the ghost
> And suffer'd pain no more.

> 'Tis finish'd, 'Tis finish'd — the Messiah dies
> For sins, but not his own;
> The great redemption is complete,
> And Satan's pow'r o'erthrown.

> 'Tis finish'd, 'Tis finish'd — all his groans are past;
> His blood, his pain and toils
> Have fully vanquished our foes,
> And crown'd him with their spoils.

'Tis finish'd, 'Tis finish'd — legal worship ends
And gospel ages run;
All old things now are past away,
And a new world begun.

(Scottish Paraphrases)

Dereliction and distress give way to dominion. It is a dominion of identification and expansion, perfectly completed on the cross. The suffering Messiah of Psalm 22 has finished his work in triumph. The dying victim provides eternal life for those who trust in him. The key to all is through Christ's substitution: calling, justification, adoption, satisfaction, healing, covering and now, finally, victory — a victory through suffering, a victory gained through Christ's apparent defeat on Calvary. Psalm 22 unlocks all these precious truths, for the New Testament story of Jesus' death goes back, again and again, to these prophetic words of David in the psalm. The dying victim of Psalm 22 is the glorious victor on the cross.

5.
Perfect Sacrifice

Psalm 40 is a song of praise for deliverance. David recalls his experience in detail:

> 'He lifted me out of the slimy pit,
>   out of the mud and mire;
> he set my feet on a rock
>   and gave me a firm place to stand'
>
> (v. 2).

He celebrates God's goodness with gratitude:

> 'Many, O Lord my God,
>   are the wonders you have done.
> The things you planned for us
>   no one can recount to you'
>
> (v. 5).

He reflects deeply on the lessons he has learned:

> 'Sacrifice and offering you did not desire...
> I desire to do your will, O my God;
>   your law is within my heart'
>
> (vv. 6,8).

He affirms publicly his trust in God:

> 'I proclaim righteousness in the great assembly...

I do not conceal your love and your truth
    from the great assembly'

                                  (vv. 9-10).

Finally, he pleads earnestly, in fresh difficulties, for a repetition
of his deliverance:

'Do not withhold your mercy from me, O Lord;
    may your love and your truth always protect me'

                                  (v. 11).

The lessons David learned are the highlight of the psalm. This is
the portion quoted in the New Testament in reference to Christ:

'Sacrifice and offering you did not desire,
    but my ears you have pierced;
burnt offerings and sin offerings
    you did not require.
Then I said, "Here I am, I have come—
    it is written about me in the scroll.
I desire to do your will, O my God;
    your law is within my heart"'

                      (Ps. 40:6-8; cf. Heb. 10:5-7).

David both sees and proclaims with vision. He is a true seer, a real
prophet of God. He shows the same insight as he grapples with his
sin of adultery in Psalm 51:

'You do not delight in sacrifice, or I would bring it;
    you do not take pleasure in burnt offerings.
The sacrifices of God are a broken spirit;
    a broken and contrite heart,
    O God, you will not despise'

                      (Ps. 51:16-17).

The lesson David learns is about sacrifice. Sacrifice is inner, not
outward; a matter of the heart rather than the hand. Yet human
sacrifice, however pure, is imperfect. It calls for divine fulfilment.
The joy of deliverance (Ps. 40) and the gloom of penitence (Ps. 51)
both point David in the same direction. His discovery of the perfect

sacrifice is an exciting find. This lies at the heart of the psalm and points to fulfilment in Christ.

A worthy response

The response David makes to his deliverance is a worthy one. The sacrifice David offers is far in excess of the normal run of religion. It is a decisively inner and personal offering. In that, David's perception is deep and peers far into the future:

> 'Sacrifice and offering you did not desire,
>   but my ears you have pierced;
> burnt offerings and sin offerings
>   you did not require'

(Ps. 40:6).

The memory of Saul's downfall would still have been fresh in David's mind. Saul had not heeded God's command. Spoils of war had been offered in sacrifice. Samuel was clear in his denunciation: to obey was better than sacrifice, to listen to God than the fat of rams. God rejected Saul as king for this disobedience. David had ample opportunity to reflect on this, daily at morning and evening sacrifice, weekly and monthly at new moon feasts, annually at the high days in the temple. David would be careful not to make the same mistake as Saul. David recalls the variety of those sacrifices: the peace offering with its reconciling meal; the grain offering with its gratitude for daily bounty; the whole burnt offering, a vow of complete dedication to God; the guilt offering to cover the offence of sin. But more was needed. Even the sin and guilt offerings only dealt with unintentional sin, not with offences committed in conscious disobedience. Sacrifices were only tokens, outer signs of inner grace. What could give David's raging conscience peace as he thought about his affair with Bathsheba? What was a worthy response to God for his mighty act of deliverance? Certainly not mere outward ceremonial. David grasps what the prophet Hosea later proclaimed of God's requirements: 'For I desire mercy, not sacrifice, and acknowledgement of God rather than burnt offerings' (Hosea 6:6).

True religion is an inward, not an outward affair. It begins with a proper attitude to God in the heart. Only then does it spread effectively to the life. No amount of religious ritual or ceremonial observance, however sincerely performed, can take the place of this. What Hosea, Isaiah, Jeremiah, Amos and all the other prophets condemned was not the system of sacrifice but its abuse: making a fetish of the animal, creating an idol of the altar. David realized the need for an inner, not an outward response to God. That alone was worthy of God's salvation.

An obedient response

Obedience was necessary. Repentance was needed. Heartfelt brokenness of life before God was required. Unrestrained and unambiguous contrition of spirit as a sinner before God was involved. There must be a willingness about this obedience too — a volition of mind, an openness of heart, a delight in self-giving. The remarkable thing David discovered is that God not only requires this; he gives it as well:

'But my ears you have pierced...
Then I said, "Here I am, I have come—
    it is written about me in the scroll.
I desire to do your will, O my God"'

(Ps. 40:6-8).

Again, David had an opportunity to reflect on this. The year of jubilee was a grand occasion, with all its gladness, including the freeing of slaves. That was not the only occasion of liberation. David knew the ceremony well — the offer of freedom; the consideration of the matter by the slave and his family; the frequently negative response; the slave brought to the door; the lobe of his ear pierced with an awl into the woodwork; the solemn words of commitment: 'I love my master; I will not go free.'

God had done that for David. God had turned to David, heard his cry, lifted him out of the slimy pit, the mud and the mire, set his feet on a rock, put a new song on his lips. Many saw this and turned to David's God for deliverance. David did not want his freedom, not if that involved leaving God. He loved his Master; he would not go free. That was the only fitting response David could make.

God had done even more for David. God had not only pierced David's ear; he had opened it as well. Indeed, God was opening up all of David's being in responsive love to his Master. David was willing and delighted to do what God wanted. The law required this of all men, including David. In that sense, David was written into the scroll of God's purpose, inscribed in God's law book. The problem for David, as for all men, was fulfilling God's law. But now God was working even towards that end. God was making David willing in the day of his power. God was bringing about an obedience to himself in David's life, a brokenness of heart, a yielded life. God, who delivered David from distress, was dedicating him to service. God was both saving and sanctifying his servant, and David knew it.

This insight again looks forward. David experiences what was later said of Isaiah's servant:

'The Sovereign Lord has opened my ears
    and I have not been rebellious;
I have not drawn back'

(Isa. 50:5).

God not only redeems from sin, but also prepares for service. David, in a remarkable way, was discovering this. How great to know God's glorious work of opening up our ears, hearts and lives to his saving purposes! David, too, in finding this, anticipates not only the worth, but the obedience of Christ's sacrifice.

An effective response

The gratifying thing about this worthy and obedient response of David is its effectiveness. It really works. David states the reason for this simply, yet profoundly: 'Your law is within my heart' (Ps. 40:8). Because the intent and purpose of God's law has penetrated David's inner being, he regards this mighty act of God's deliverance and the response in his life as effective. God has really dealt with the problem in David's life in a vital way, lifting him from hopelessness, stabilizing his existence, preparing his heart for obedience and his life for service.

David again acts as a prophet. His experience previews God's promise given later by Jeremiah that God would establish a new covenant relationship with his people by writing his law on their hearts:

> "'This is the covenant that I will make with the house of
>   Israel
>   after that time," declares the Lord.
> "I will put my law in their minds
>   and write it on their hearts.
> I will be their God,
>   and they will be my people'"

(Jer. 31:33).

A sufficient offering

All of David's insights into the worth, obedience and effectiveness of a true response to God's salvation point forward to Christ's perfect sacrifice. The truth about our hopelessness in sin, our need of deliverance, the joy of God's purpose in our hearts and the power of God's direction for our lives is all present here. David sees that deliverance, not through outward religious forms or ceremonial, but by an inner work of God's grace. The God-ordained sacrifices around him pointed to this. Indeed, perhaps they pointed forward to the worthy, obedient and effective sacrifice of the Messiah himself. David looked forward and, however dimly, glimpsed this. We who look back to Christ's sacrifice and appropriate it by faith can begin to discover David's experience of God's grace in our own lives.

Some take the whole of Psalm 40 as Messianic. In that case, it recalls God's deliverance of Christ in his distress, tells of the Son's love and devotion for the Father and echoes Jesus' pleadings in his agony on the cross. The problem of the psalmist's self-conscious-ness of sin — 'My sins have overtaken me, and I cannot see' (Ps. 40:12) — as referring to Christ is explained on the ground of Christ's bearing our sins as our substitute. The writer to the Hebrews, however, focuses directly on verses 6-8. He stresses the finality of

Christ's death as a sacrifice for sin. He quotes these verses and
expounds them with this end in view. His exposition shows the
fulfilment of David's worthy, obedient and effective response to
God for deliverance in Christ's perfect sacrifice on Calvary.

A superior sacrifice

The *worth* of David's response is fulfilled in the superiority of
Christ's self-offering:

'Therefore when Christ came into the world, he said,

"Sacrifice and offering you did not desire,
   but a body you prepared for me;
with burnt offerings and sin offerings
   you were not pleased.
Then I said, 'Here I am — it is written about me in the
      scroll—
I have come to do your will, O God.'"

'First he said, "Sacrifices and offerings, burnt offerings
and sin offerings you did not desire, nor were you pleased
with them" (although the law required them to be made). Then
he said, "Here I am, I have come to do your will." He sets aside
the first to establish the second'

(Heb. 10:5-9).

The apostle views the superiority of Christ's sacrifice in terms of
abolition and fulfilment. Christ sets aside the sacrificial system of
the old dispensation in its entirety, to establish a new regime based
on the one and only sacrifice of himself. As David perceives the only
worthy response to God, not in outward religious acts but in inner
self-giving, Christ sets aside the animal offerings in the temple by
his own self-oblation on Calvary. Christ's sacrifice is worthy, for it
is superior.

The idea of superiority over outward sacrificial ceremonial
appears in Jesus' ministry from the very outset. It was accomplished
by a process of abolition and fulfilment too. This was Jesus'
expressed intention for his kingdom at his baptism. Confronted by

John, who was reluctant that Jesus should receive a baptism of repentance for the forgiveness of sins, Jesus nevertheless insisted. It was necessary in this way to 'fulfil all righteousness'. Jesus would identify with sinners by receiving a sinner's baptism, for ultimately he was to die as a sacrifice for sin. He would thus abolish sin and establish righteousness. His sacrifice is far in excess of the old animal sacrifices.

Superiority is clear in Jesus' teaching about the kingdom. He explained it to his disciples in terms of abolishing the old and establishing the new. In teaching the new law of the kingdom, Jesus claims that he has come not to abolish the law and the prophets but to fulfil them. Yet obviously he abolishes something: 'You have heard that it was said to the people long ago... But I tell you.' What is it Jesus abolishes? It is certainly not the law and the prophets, for Jesus establishes the inner intent of the law about murder, adultery, divorce, oaths and retaliation. It is rather the misconstructions, misinterpretations, additions and omissions put on the law by the religious teachers, which Jesus abolishes. He does this to fulfil and to establish the law and the prophets. He reclaims the true meaning by exposing the abuse. Therein lies the superiority of the new law over the old. It exceeds outward ceremonial or formal assent or misinterpretation. It offers a better way.

In this superiority, however, Jesus also abolishes what is God-given but waxing old. The apostles see the superiority of Jesus' teaching in this light. Paul writes, 'He has made us competent as ministers of a new covenant — not of the letter but of the Spirit; for the letter kills, but the Spirit gives life... For what was glorious has no glory now in comparison with the surpassing glory. And if what was fading away came with glory, how much greater is the glory of that which lasts!' (2 Cor. 3:6,10,11).

The writer to the Hebrews expresses the same truth like this: 'By calling this covenant "new", he has made the first one obsolete; and what is obsolete and ageing will soon disappear' (Heb. 8:13).

This superiority becomes more evident as opposition to the kingdom grows. When Jesus calls Matthew from his tax-collector's booth and shares a meal to celebrate with Matthew's friends, angry Pharisees complain to Jesus' disciples that their rabbi keeps company with tax collectors and 'sinners'. When, later, the disciples are hungry on the Sabbath day and pluck some ears of corn to eat, the Pharisees, equally bitter, charge them with breaking the Sabbath.

On both occasions Jesus replies by quoting the prophet Hosea: 'I desire mercy not sacrifice' (Matt. 9:13; 12:7; cf. Hosea 6:6). Jesus shows that God requires a better form of response than mere outward ceremonial or perfunctory observance. The intents and purposes of the heart are involved. The motive behind the action is important, whether this means recognizing one's own sin or the needs of others.

Jesus makes the same point when he criticizes the teachers of the law for giving tithes of mint, anise and cummin but neglecting the weightier issues of justice and righteousness. They strain at a gnat but swallow a camel. There is a better way than that.

The superiority of Jesus' teaching reaches its climax in the evangelism of the kingdom. Towards the close of his ministry, Jesus is encouraged by the approach of a well-intentioned lawyer, who notes the good answers Jesus gives to the teachers of the law. On hearing Jesus' reply to his question regarding the most important of the commandments, the lawyer responds: 'Well said, teacher… You are right in saying that God is one and there is no other but him. To love him with all your heart, with all your understanding and with all your strength, and to love your neighbour as yourself is more important than all burnt offerings and sacrifices' (Mark 12:32-33).

That reply closed the public debate. From then on, no one dared ask Jesus any more questions (Mark 12:34). The reply went to the heart of the matter. That was the true essence of the kingdom, for that was the inner intent of God's law. Jesus eventually fulfilled the inner intent of the sacrificial system by abolishing its outward form through the sacrifice of himself. What the law was incapable of doing because of the sinful nature, the Son of God did by his own self-offering (Rom. 8:3). There is therefore no more place for animal sacrifice. Christ's worthy and superior self-sacrifice removes the need for it (Heb. 10:8). Jesus fulfils the law by abolishing animal sacrifices in the superior sacrifice of himself once for all for sin.

This brings us to the very heart of Christ's message. Entering Christ's kingdom does not consist of outward form but inner grace. It is not a matter of religious ceremonial but of personal brokenness; not an accumulation of human sacrifices making the worshipper worthy, but an acceptance of Christ's sacrifice as an atonement for sin. Only after entering the kingdom in this way are the offerings of good works acceptable. The sacrifices of God are a broken and a contrite heart.

Elizabeth appeared outwardly to be a Christian. She was a communicant member of the church. Later, she and her husband came to personal faith in Christ. It was completely different then. She saw her former stance to have been one of mere outward ceremonial, so much so, that she insisted on attending church membership classes and publicly professing her faith in Christ. For her, the old outward form had been abolished, a new inner grace established. The visible tokens of her professed faith remained the same — baptism and the Lord's Supper — but the signs were now invested with a meaning she had never known before. Faith replaced religion, grace superseded works, personal experience ousted ceremonial observance. She came to know a better way — the worth and superiority of Christ's perfect sacrifice.

Not all the blood of beasts,
On Jewish altars slain,
Could give the guilty conscience peace
Or wash away the stain.

But Christ, the heavenly Lamb,
Takes all our sins away;
A sacrifice of nobler name
And richer blood than they.

My faith would lay her hand
On that dear head of thine
While like a penitent I stand,
And there confess my sin.

Believing, we rejoice
To see the curse remove;
We bless the Lamb with cheerful voice
And sing his bleeding love.

(Isaac Watts)

A willing sacrifice

The *obedience* of David's response finds ultimate fulfilment in the willing nature of Christ's sacrifice. In expounding this part of Psalm

40, the writer to the Hebrews stresses how readily Christ offered himself in death:

> "'…but a body you prepared for me…
> Then I said, 'Here I am — it is written about me in the
>   scroll—
> I have come to do your will, O God'"…

> 'Then he said, "Here I am, I have come to do your will." He sets aside the first to establish the second. And by that will, we have been made holy'
>
> (Heb. 10:5-7,9-10).

Christ's willingness is seen in his obedient self-sacrifice. It is through Christ's will that the body prepared by God for his Son is offered. The compulsion which leads to Calvary does not rest, in the final analysis, on political intrigue or force of circumstances, but on Christ's inner motivation, his willingness to die. David found his whole being opening up in obedient response to God. Christ experiences something similar. Compelling passion and yielding subservience to God control his will and impel him forward in self-sacrifice.

John Owen expresses this well: 'Secondly, the Son was an *agent* in this great work, concurring by a voluntary susception, or willing undertaking of the office imposed on him; for when the Lord said, "Sacrifice and offering he would not: in burnt-offerings and sacrifices for sin he had no pleasure," then said Christ, "Lo, I come, (in the volume of the book it is written of me), to do thy will, O God," Heb.10:6,7… He might have been cruciated on the part of God; but his death could not have been an oblation and offering had not his will concurred.'

The writer to the Hebrews quotes from the Greek version of the Old Testament, where we find, 'But a body you prepared for me', which in the Hebrew version is 'But my ears you have pierced.' The Greek translation is really an interpretation of the literal Hebrew: 'Ears you dug for me,' where the sense is taken to mean not so much the piercing of the ears but rather the hollowing out of them, which is part of the total work of fashioning a human body. The overall sense is plain: God works in David's life to produce in him a willing obedience, preparing, shaping, moulding him for service. The apostle picks up this theme in his exposition: God's preparation of a body for his Son leads to Christ's willingness to offer his body in sacrifice. Christ's prepared body anticipates his willing obedience in sacrifice. Love for the Father's goodness compels the Son's ready response.

Willing obedience marks the whole of Jesus' life but it becomes more obvious as the cross approaches. Events from midway through the ministry reflect the growing intensity of Jesus' will towards self-sacrifice. Mark recalls how, after Peter's confession, Jesus began to teach his disciples that the Son of Man must suffer many things at the hands of the chief priests and rulers of the people, how he would be crucified and on the third day would rise from the dead (Mark 8:31). The instruction is continuing, systematic and specific: the Son of Man came not to be served but to serve and to give his life a ransom for many (Mark 9:12,31; 10:45).

Luke traces this determination even in Jesus' demeanour. Jesus sets his face like a flint to go to Jerusalem (Luke 9:51). The shadow of the cross is cast in these events. They preview Calvary. John records how Jesus explains that his food is to do God's will (John 4:27-38), and that Jesus lays down his life voluntarily (John 10:17-18). Jesus determines of his own volition to obey his Father in sacrificing his life for the sheep.

Gethsemane is a high point in Jesus' willing obedience (Matt. 26:36-46; Mark 14:32-42; Luke 22:39-46). There on his face before his Father, the Son yields in absolute submission. Christ, for whom God prepared a body, comes in total surrender to do God's will. What condescension is there — the eternal Son enters the realm of finite possibility, for the cup could conceivably pass from him. What self-sacrifice is there — the will of God the Father involves the orphaned dereliction of his sin-bearing Son. What love is there — Christ drains the cup of wrath to the dregs that we might drink the cup of blessing to overflowing. What human loneliness is there — Jesus returns yet again to find his friends asleep. No wonder Jesus shook and shuddered as he looked into the abyss of his Gethsemane experience.

Gethsemane was the battleground for Jesus' will. There, his will was rebroken and refashioned in surrendered obedience. That accomplished, Calvary was inevitable. Earlier in the wilderness, the protagonist was Satan. That was fearful. Here in the garden, he faced his Father. This was horrendous. Yet peace came — the peace of

coming to do God's will whatever it involved; the peace of even
delighting in doing God's will; the peace of knowing that God was
making him willing in the day of his power, preparing a body,
completing the law-scroll, doing God's will. Gethsemane, followed
by Calvary, is the ultimate fulfilment of Psalm 40:7-8.

> 'Then I said, "Here I am, I have come—
>   it is written about me in the scroll.
> I desire to do your will, O my God;
>   your law is within my heart."'

Joni Eareckson Tada is a household name in Christian circles,
particularly where suffering is involved. At seventeen she was a
victim of a diving accident, and as a result became a quadriplegic,
severely paralysed. Her story, as she faced this tragedy as a Christian, is intriguing and inspiring. Gethsemanes litter her life. The path
of suffering and of struggling to cope with her disability, not only
physically but psychologically, is the story of her faith. She describes it with a stark plainness that boggles the mind.

The early Gethsemane of shock threw her into confusion. Why
had God let this happen to her? She professed to be a Christian, but
now she wondered, was there a God at all? She read Sartre and Marx
but found no help. From shock she turned back to the Bible.

The Gethsemane of despair plagued her life. Hopes of healing
were dashed to pieces on the rocks of unremitting paralysis. Prayer
was unanswered for her on that score. She resented this and turned
to self-pity, but Scripture and Christian friends gave her hope amid
the gloom. At first she would not write with a pen in her mouth but,
eventually, she came to express artistic skills by that very method.
God was turning her valley of Achor into a door of hope.

The Gethsemane of shattered relationships brought her
heartache. Apart from the simple things of never being able to comb
her hair or put make-up on her face, she entertained the possibility
of marriage, only to have her hopes swept away just when she began
to feel like a woman again. But God rescued her and gave her
strength and vision. What saw Joni through this frightful
experience?

Some words from her book *Start of a Journey* show how God
prepared her shattered body and produced in her a willing obedience
through a Son's love and a Father's sovereignty:

'I discovered that the Lord Jesus Christ could indeed empathize with my situation. On the cross for those agonizing horrible hours, waiting for death. He was immobilized, helpless, paralysed...

'Jesus did know what it was like not to be able to move — not to be able to scratch your nose, shift your weight, wipe your eyes. He was paralysed on the cross. He could not move His arms or legs. Christ knew exactly how I felt! ...

'Wisdom is *trusting* God, not asking "Why, God?" Relaxed and in God's will, I know He is in control. It is not a blind, stubborn, stoic acceptance but getting to know God and realize He is worthy of my trust. Although I am fickle and play games, God does not. Although I have been up and down, bitter and doubting, He is constant, ever loving...

'My mind has roamed back through the scenes of the past eight years. Familiar faces of family and friends came to mind ... people God has brought into my life to help bend and mould me more closely to Christ's image... All of it has been part of "growing in grace". The girl who became emotionally distraught and wavered at each new set of circumstances is now grown up, a woman who has learned to rely on God's sovereignty.'

Because Christ faced Gethsemane and offered his prepared body to his Father on the cross, Joni was transformed from being a fearful, doubting girl into a mature Christian woman. Her example moves us as Christians to follow Christ to Gethsemane in total submission of our wills to the will of God.

The final sacrifice

The *effectiveness* of David's experience is realized in the finality of Christ's sacrifice. David found God's work in his life to be truly effective: God opened David's ears to hear his Word. He filled David's life and brought him to offer willing service. God did this by placing his law in David's heart. The renewal of David's inner life by the impress of God's law on his heart was the real cause of his worthy and obedient response to God. In that sense, it was amazingly effective and it was totally of grace.

David anticipates the work of the covenant of grace in the life of the believer here. David had always been conscious of God's covenant promise, both to him personally as king and corporately as head of God's people. At this point, he anticipates the fulfilment of God's 'new covenant' proclaimed by Jeremiah hundreds of years later:

> 'I will put my law in their minds,
>   and write it on their hearts.
> I will be their God
>   and they will be my people'

(Jer. 31:33).

David anticipates this in Psalm 40 in a double sense: he predicts the superior sacrifice of Christ, but he also forecasts the perfect nature of the Christ who offers the sacrifice. He foretells Christ both as high priest and as sacrifical victim. David may have experienced the effectiveness of God's law written on his own heart, but it is a pale reflection of what he predicts concerning Christ. Christ alone has God's law written perfectly on his heart. As such, his sacrificial offering is effective and final. Christ is both perfect sacrifice and perfect priest.

This is the aspect of Psalm 40 which the apostle to the Hebrews notes in conclusion. He does so, too, precisely in the terms in which David experienced the prophecy. The writer to the Hebrews emphasizes the effectiveness of Christ's sacrifice through its finality. It is a 'once-for-all' offering, a complete, finished work. In this it contrasts with the sacrifices of the temple. They were endlessly repetitive. They dealt only with ceremonial uncleanness. They were ineffective in removing the root and cause of sin. It was impossible for the blood of bulls and goats to take away sin. The worshipper still felt guilty. At this point, the apostle quotes Psalm 40:6-8 to show the superior nature of Christ's sacrifice, as prophesied by David. He omits those words in the psalm, 'Your law is within my heart' (Ps. 40:8), but he affirms their truth through the willing sacrifice of Christ: 'And by that will, we have been made holy through the sacrifice of the body of Jesus Christ once for all' (Heb. 10:10).

The effectiveness of Christ's sacrifice through its finality produces sanctification in the believer. The believer is made holy, as a completed, finished work through the finished work of Christ. His conscience is cleansed from sin, the law of God is written upon his heart and the covenant of grace is realized in his life.

The writer explains the results of this effectiveness also through the finality of Christ's priesthood. Day after day the priest stands and offers the same sacrifices, which can never take away sins. Christ, after he had offered for all time one sacrifice for sins, sat down at the right hand of God's majesty. The priest had always to stand while officiating at the altar. It was a mark of his duty. That Christ should offer himself once for all and then sit down at God's right hand stressed both the finality and effectiveness of what he had done as priest. Both priest and victim are marked by perfection: 'Since that time he waits for his enemies to be made his footstool, because by one sacrifice he has made perfect for ever those who are being made holy' (Heb. 10:13-14).

The believer's sanctification is doubly secured by both priest and victim. The one sacrifice by the perfect priest renders the believer perfect for ever. There could be no higher index of the completeness of the offering than that. The practical effect of the sacrifice is evident in the continuing process of sanctification in those who are already perfected by Christ's priestly work. Those who are already 'perfect' are being made 'perfect' by both priest and victim.

To drive this point home, the apostle quotes Jeremiah 31:33-34. The experience of David, the prophecy of Jeremiah and the work of Christ are all of a piece. Covenant promise and fulfilment ensure not only the effectiveness and finality of Christ's offering, but the end of temple sacrifice for ever.

'The Holy Spirit also testifies to us about this. First he says:

'"This is the covenant I will make with them
    after that time, says the Lord.
I will put my laws in their hearts,
    and I will write them on their minds."

'Then he adds:

"Their sins and lawless acts
    I will remember no more."

'And where these have been forgiven, there is no longer any
sacrifice for sin'

(Heb. 10:15-18; cf. Jer. 31:33-34).

James Denny expresses the finality of Christ's death in Hebrews
superbly: 'This is certainly not the view of the writer to the Hebrews.
On the contrary, he has, like Paul and others to whom reference has
been, and will yet be made, the conception of a *finished work* of
Christ, a work finished in His death, something done in regard to sin
once for all, whether any given soul responds to it or not. As he puts
it at the beginning of the Epistle, He made purgation of sins — the
thing was done — before He sat down at the right hand of the
Majesty in the Heavens. As he puts it later, He has offered one
sacrifice for sins for ever, and by the one offering He has brought for
ever into the perfect relation to God those who are being sanctified.'

John Owen, with equal clarity, makes the point that the finality
of Christ's death and the effectiveness implicit in this finality is
evident in the sanctification in the lives of those for whom Christ
died: atonement is not universal but particular and limited in that
sense. Only that view is worthy of the finality and effectiveness of
Christ's death: 'If the blood of Jesus Christ doth *wash, purge,
cleanse* and *sanctify* them for whom it was shed, or for whom he was
a sacrifice, then certainly he died, shed his blood, or was a sacrifice,
only for them that in the event are *washed, purged, cleansed* and
sanctified… Sanctification and holiness is the certain fruit and
effect of the death of Christ in all them for whom he died; but all and
every one are not partakers of this sanctification, this purging,
cleansing and working of holiness: therefore Christ died not for all
and every one, *"quod erat demonstrandum"*.'

Jesus experiences what David foretells and the apostle to the
Hebrews recalls. Jesus gives three pictures of his death which
underline this effective finality. His death is a *baptism* he must
undergo and he is under stress until it is accomplished (Luke 12:49-
50). It is a *cup* he must drink and he must drain it to the bitter dregs
(Matt. 26:39,42). It is a *ransom-price* he must pay and, in doing so,
he sacrifices himself totally (Mark 10:45). All these images pervade
Jesus' mind as the end approaches. He is not only made willing for
God's purpose, he senses the effective, if awful, finality of the action
which lies before him. So when, on the cross, he commits his spirit
ultimately to God his Father, it is not the pathetic cry of a defeated

and deluded mortal. When he utters the word 'Finished!', it is not as a drudge, who reluctantly rids himself of some troublesome burden. It is rather the cry of a Son, who has obediently completed his Father's will. It is the voice of victory, not defeat; of triumph, not despair. For Jesus, the sacrifice of his life was a final and effective culmination of his entire ministry. The torn curtain in the temple and the raised dead walking about Jerusalem were living proof of its effectiveness and finality.

Jesus is self-consciously not only victim but priest as well, and, as priest, he is very aware of the need to finalize the work his Father has committed to him: 'Father, the time has come, glorify your Son, that your Son may glorify you' (John 17:1). 'I have brought you glory on earth by completing the work you gave me to do' (John 17:4). 'I have given them the glory that you gave me, that they may be one as we are one: I in them and you in me. May they be brought to complete unity to let the world know that you sent me and have loved them even as you have loved me' (John 17:22-23).

Jesus the great High Priest finishes the work his Father has called him to do — he completes his priestly office with finality and effectiveness. His work is perfect, as both priest and victim, for it is final. This is the scenario in which Jesus cries, 'Finished!'

The glory of this truth should never be lost on us. It is the clarion cry of victory of the Christian gospel — the finished work of Christ. Whether it is the self-righteous, religious person, brought up within the pale of Christendom, trusting in good works but having no peace of conscience; or the optimistic restorationist, who needs to realize that a rebuilt temple and reconstituted sacrifices are an unbiblical pipe-dream; or the reluctant son of Judaism, who must be convinced that Messiah has come and, in one fell swoop, has both fulfilled and abolished the sacrifices; or the baleful Muslim to whom we proclaim that Jesus the Son of God has done all, so Mohammed and the Koran are redundant; or the restless Hindu, who needs to find complete and final rebirth in Christ, rather than in endless reincarnations in some future existence; or the hopeful New Ager who must accept that God is not dead and the answer lies not in the force of man but in the power of Christ — the message is still the same: the finished work of Christ, the Son of God, is the final and effective solution to all man's need. It is a finished, completed and perfect work. The exclusive uniqueness of Jesus' person is evident in the finished nature of his work. He is the way, the truth and the life, and that exclusively. No one comes to God but through Christ. This needs to be stressed in days of so-called 'inter-faith dialogue' with non-Christian religions. There is no common ground. Jesus' uniqueness sweeps away any thought of this. Individual Christians and the corporate church of Christ must relearn this lesson and proclaim it with authority as the unique and only gospel.

David's worthy response in Psalm 40 anticipates Christ's superior sacrifice. David's obedient life previews Christ's willing self-giving. David's effective discovery augurs Christ's finished work. Hundreds of years before it happened David foretold it — a perfect sacrifice, superior, willing, final: a perfect sacrifice by a perfect priest. The perfection, as the Greek word suggests, lies in its completed quality. It sanctifies *for ever* those who are being sanctified. The covenant of grace is fulfilled, God's law is in man's heart through Jesus the perfect sacrifice.

6.
Risen Lord

In some psalms, David praises God's greatness as Creator and Redeemer. In others, he prays to God for deliverance. Sometimes he grows angry and calls down vengeance on his enemies. Psalm 16 is different. It is reflective, calm yet passionate. David scans his experience — past, present and future. He relaxes for a moment from the heat of his fevered life to focus on God and all that God has done for him. Scenes from various parts of his life flash into his mind. He recounts, absorbs and comments on them. But there is a connecting link. It is God's goodness, his faithfulness, his covenant love which binds all together. This gives meaning to the varied scenes of the past. It persuades David of God's purpose in the present. It predicts security and hope, even eternity of life, for the future.

The concept of the covenant is not only the key to David's thoughts in Psalm 16; it is the door to understanding the unfolding story of the whole Old Testament. A covenant was an agreement based on a promise between two parties. David and Jonathan made a covenant of friendship and their pact rested on mutual trust. Perhaps the best modern example of a covenant is marriage: a man and woman promise lifelong fidelity to each other as they take their marriage vows. They promise and covenant to be loving, faithful and dutiful to one another.

The term 'covenant' is used throughout the Old Testament to describe God's relationship with Israel. Here the situation is different, for the covenant is not between equals but between a superior, God, and an inferior, man. God takes the initiative in establishing his covenant, promising certain benefits to his people and requiring certain obligations of them. This is the saga of salvation in the Old Testament.

God called Abraham to leave Ur in Mesopotamia and established his covenant with him and with his descendants (Gen. 12:1-2). God renewed his covenant with Moses at the exodus from Egypt and at the giving of the law on Sinai, when the tribe had become a nation (Exod. 24:1-8). God confirmed his covenant to David, promising him a stable dynasty and hinting at a future Messiah as king (2 Sam. 7:11-16). God announced his covenant through Isaiah, telling of a child-king who would rule over an everlasting kingdom and through Jeremiah, predicting a 'new covenant' that would place God's law in men's minds, causing them to know him and effectively forgiving all their sins (Isa. 9:6-7; Jer. 31:31-34).

The New Testament is the fulfilment of this covenant theme in the birth, death and resurrection of Christ. Mary celebrates her pregnancy as God helping his servant Israel and remembering to be merciful to Abraham and his descendants (Luke 1:54-55). Jesus describes his death as the blood of the new covenant shed for many for the forgiveness of sins (Matt. 26:28). The writer to the Hebrews views the resurrection as the God of peace bringing Jesus back from death through the blood of the eternal covenant (Heb. 13:20). What the Old Testament says expansively of God's covenant, Psalm 16 portrays in microcosm from David's own experience. Covenant lies behind David's thoughts in Psalm 16 — past, present and future.

Past

David reflects on God as his refuge — something he often does. God is his shelter, his fortress, his high tower. But the exclusive nature of that protection grips him in this instance. Apart from God, he has no good thing. He ponders the blessings of God's people, of whom he is one. He delights in being one of their number, sharing fellowship with them. There is glory in that.

David deplores the pagan idolaters around him. He sees them run after their gods, pour out their drink offerings to them, incant their demonic names in endless repetition. He will have none of that. His past has taught him one thing, at least. The lines of demarcation between God's people and others are clearly drawn. This warm, personal relationship with the covenant God which David shares with God's people is all that matters. Exclusive commitment to the covenant-making Jehovah is the heartbeat of life. That alone makes sense of the past.

'Keep me safe, O God,
　　for in you I take refuge.
I said to the Lord, "You are my Lord;
　　apart from you I have no good thing."
As for the saints who are in the land,
　　they are the glorious ones in whom is all my delight.
The sorrows of those will increase
　　who run after other gods.
I will not pour out their libations of blood
　　or take up their names on my lips'

(Ps. 16:1-4).

Present

The present is equally secure in the purpose of God. God pours out the allotted cup of life for David to drink. David often thought of life in that way. God makes the wicked drink a cup of foaming wine mixed with spices down to the very dregs (Ps. 75:8). But David's cup is overflowing (Ps. 23:5). It is the cup of God's salvation (Ps. 116:13). Here David thinks of how that cup is apportioned by God just for him for each particular circumstance, for every event that comes his way. God's 'cup' is his purpose for David in the present.

An inherited 'land' was another way of thinking about that purpose. David knew this was truly a covenant theme. To Abraham's successors God had promised a land, willed it to them by inheritance. Joseph may have lain embalmed in a coffin in Egypt, but eventually God's people came back to that promised land under Moses. Joshua helped them possess it. Judges helped them govern it. Now, under David's kingship, the boundaries of that land had reached their furthest extent, from the Euphrates in the north to Egypt in the south. God had done this for David. His present, as his past, was a covenant blessing, an allotted cup, an apportioned land:

'Lord, you have assigned me my portion and my cup;
　　you have made my lot secure.
The boundary lines have fallen for me in pleasant places;
　　surely I have a delightful inheritance'

(Ps. 16:5-6).

Future

God's covenant love for David in the past and present made him
confident. It would secure even his future. David puts this in a
striking way: God keeps David's heart. His innermost thoughts are
controlled by God. His deepest passions are stirred by the divine
will. Even subconsciously, as he sleeps, God instructs him. God
orders David's actions. With God at his right hand, he will never be
moved. God prompts David's speech. His tongue sings praises out
of a glad heart. In thought, word and deed the covenant God ordains
David's future. It is safe in God's hands.

Most remarkably of all, David's body will be safe too. God will
not abandon him to the separation of the grave. God will not allow
corruption ultimately to destroy him. Pleasure and joy in the
presence of God, and that to an eternal degree, will be David's fate
rather than the awful chasm and putrefying decay of death. In a
strange way, David grasps as an individual what Job anticipated.
Though worms destroy his body, yet in his flesh he would see God
(Job 19:26). David saw what Daniel predicted of all mankind. There
would be a general resurrection, some to everlasting life, others to
everlasting shame and contempt (Dan. 12:2). David prophesied
what Isaiah foretold of the servant Messiah. After the suffering of
his soul, he would see the light of life and be satisfied (Isa. 53:11).
There was hope beyond the grave. There was an afterlife. God's
covenant, which secured David's past and present in thought, word
and deed, would preserve his entire being, even his body, into the
future. There would be no ultimate decay, no final abandonment, but
pleasures for him at God's right hand for evermore. This was the
future for all the righteous through the covenant promise and the
covenant Messiah of God. This was the climax of all blessings, and
David would share that blessing too. Why did David think like this?
What moved his meditations in this direction? What gave him this
perception?

David thought of his whole life, his body included, as inextricably bound up with God's covenant promise. Towards the end of his
life as he lay on the dusty battlefield, it came to mind again (2 Sam.
23:13-17). The Philistine garrison was encamped over the hillside
and, in the brief respite from fighting, David again had time to
reflect. How God had blessed him: the Philistines were still a foe, but
a broken force, a spent power. The extent of his kingdom was firmly

established in spite of Absalom's rebellion and other opposition. The many mighty men he had, as he scanned their hardened faces but knew their true hearts, assured him of this. How thirsty he was! He longed for a drink from the well at Bethlehem's gate and he thought aloud.

Three of his trusty warriors broke ranks, went through the Philistine lines, filled the skins at the well and returned to their weary master. It was incredible, such courage, such faithfulness. David would not drink. He poured the water out as a drink offering to the Lord. He would not drink the blood of men who risked their lives.

Words he had just repeated came back to mind:

'Is not my house right with God?
   Has he not made with me an everlasting covenant,
   arranged and secured in every part?
Will he not bring to fruition my salvation
   and grant me my every desire?'

(2 Sam. 23:5).

This was the God whom David served and, every part of his life, even down to physical thirst, knew it — a perfection of ordering, a faithfulness of design. Ever since the day God had assured him that though he would not build the temple, God's covenant love would never leave him nor his dynasty, he had known this truth.

'You said, "I have made a covenant with my chosen one.
   I have sworn to David my servant,
'I will establish your line for ever
   and make your throne firm through all generations'"'

(Ps. 89:3-4).

God's covenant love protected past, present and future. Even his body was eternally secure. Therein lay the very essence of David's faith. It was faith in a covenant-making and a covenant-keeping God.

'I will praise the Lord, who counsels me,
   even at night my heart instructs me.
I have set the Lord always before me.

Because he is at my right hand,
I shall not be shaken.
Therefore my heart is glad and my tongue rejoices;
    my body also will rest secure,
because you will not abandon me to the grave,
    nor will you let your Holy One see decay.
You have made known to me the path of life
    you will fill me with joy in your presence
    with eternal pleasures at your right hand'

(Ps. 16:7-11).

Resurrection

The covenant blessings of Psalm 16 are supremely fulfilled in the resurrection of Christ. Both Peter and Paul make this clear. As the risen Jesus opened his disciples' minds so they could understand the Scriptures, all the details began to fit into place — the sufferings of Christ, the resurrection on the third day, the preaching of repentance and forgiveness to all nations. It confirmed Jesus' earlier teaching that everything written about him in the Law, Prophets and Psalms must be fulfilled. It excited the disciples to wait in Jerusalem for the Spirit's power. It made an indelible mark on the apostolic mind-set. It enabled them to see that the Jesus whom they would eventually proclaim was the Christ of Scripture. So when they preached, they preached in that way. Peter quoted Psalm 16:8-11 on the Day of Pentecost at Jerusalem to prove Jesus' resurrection (Acts 2:25-28). Paul cited Psalm 16:10 to the same end in the synagogue in Pisidian Antioch (Acts 13:35).

It is the similarity of apostolic witness that grips the mind as we read both these sermons with their two pointed references. It is not a similarity of common source or concocted speech, as to what Luke imagined Peter and Paul said, but a unity of mind and purpose, of passion and commitment, of understanding and perception — a unity of apostolic witness according to the Scriptures, a résumé of words Peter and Paul really did say.

The similarity covers many aspects of the two addresses. The *time* was the same, not in terms of date and hour but of occasion: Peter, restored to faith in Jesus, freshly baptized by the Spirit, proclaiming Christ at the outset of an impressive ministry; Paul, recently commissioned by the church in Judæan Antioch, excitingly successful on the island of Cyprus, invited now to address the synagogue in Pisidian Antioch on his very first missionary tour. The *setting* was similar, not as regards geographical location but audience composition: gathered Jewry at a feast in Jerusalem, assembled Israel in an outpost of the Dispersion. Above all, the *message* was the same: the Christ of Scripture, in his death, resurrection and proclamation, is Jesus of Nazareth.

The very theme of resurrection coincides. Peter will convince Jews at Jerusalem that Psalm 16:8-11 could not find ultimate fulfilment in David but in Jesus alone: 'Brothers, I can tell you confidently that the patriarch David died and was buried, and his tomb is here to this day' (Acts 2:29). Paul presents precisely the same truth in exactly the same way regarding Psalm 16:10: 'For when David had served God's purpose in his own generation, he fell asleep; he was buried with his fathers and his body decayed. But the one whom God raised from the dead did not see decay' (Acts 13:36-37).

Peter and Paul are not saying that David could never have aspired to think these thoughts, or to speak these words of resurrection about himself, but that, in tandem with that aspiration, came the inspiration of the prophet. The psalmist was here predicting something which, exactly and ultimately in its fulfilment, could not have found realization in David. David would have to await that fulfilment, along with all other believers, in David's greater Son — 'Christ the first fruits, then they that are Christ's at his coming'. What Peter and Paul are here affirming is the supremacy of David's greater Son Jesus over David himself in terms of the exact and ultimate fulfilment of this prophecy. David died, decayed and his tomb containing his bones was a visible proof of his death to that day. It is the superiority of Christ over David that the uniform message of the apostles is stressing. The apex of David's aspirations is fulfilled in Jesus' resurrection alone. The decayed remains of Jesus were never found. They did not exist.

As each apostle unfolds the resurrection, an individual emphasis emerges which blends together in a unified witness. The remarkable thing is that behind the different emphases lies the same basic truth of the covenant. It is as though Peter and Paul show us two sides of the one coin, the resurrection of Jesus from two varying angles, both converging on the covenant promise. The same conviction which led David to grasp by faith the blessing of life with God beyond death underlies the resurrection of Jesus. The covenant is the key to this glorious truth.

Resurrection according to Peter

Peter stresses the resurrection as an example of God's power, his sovereignty over the will of man. Jews at Jerusalem for Pentecost would have read recent events in terms of human history. Jesus posed a threat to Israel's religion. False messiahs there had always been. Something would have to be done. Jewish leaders appealed to Roman authorities to deal with the matter and that was an end of it. Peter, however, set events in the context of the divine will. He read history in a very different way: 'This man was handed over to you by God's set purpose and foreknowledge; and you, with the help of wicked men, put him to death by nailing him to the cross. But God raised him from the dead, freeing him from the agony of death, because it was impossible for death to keep its hold on him' (Acts 2:23-24).

This is the *sovereignty* of God's covenant. The sovereignty of God's covenant in salvation is always to the fore in Scripture. There were human covenants in the Old Testament, but God's covenant is remarkably different. As we have already seen, it is not a pact between equals but a condescending disposition made by a superior promising great benefits to an inferior. The power of the superior to confer such grace is always prominent. God gives what he promises in salvation. The resurrection is a startling example of the sovereignty of God's covenant promise. The divine will annuls human intention by sovereign power: men put Jesus to death, but God raised him to life. God's power in salvation both negates man's will and converts it to his purpose. There is a divine sovereignty at the very heart of God's covenant. Peter sees the resurrection as a confirmation of God's promise, his grace attested to sinful man.

We simply do not know what the Jews thought of Christ's resurrection. This is the intriguing thing. After the initial attempts at denial, the debate ceases and Jewish persecution replaces scepticism. The Jews had obviously failed to disprove the resurrection. They needed only to have produced the remains of Jesus, but, of course, they did not do so, because they could find no remains to produce. So they harassed rather than heckled the Christians. Peter sees their ancestral King David in a very different light and reasons against both their scepticism and persecution from their own religion: 'But he was a prophet and knew that God had promised him on oath that he would place one of his descendants on his throne. Seeing what was ahead, he spoke of the resurrection of the Christ, that he was not abandoned to the grave, nor did his body see decay. God has raised this Jesus to life, and we are all witnesses of the fact' (Acts 2:30-31).

This is the *grace* of God's covenant. Grace is basic to the covenant theme in Scripture. God's covenant is undeserved and condescending. Election is unconditional. Jesus' death was brought about in part by man's sinfulness. Man could do nothing to resolve what he had caused. God miraculously and mercifully changes the situation. Similarly, man is enslaved by sin in a fallen nature. He is powerless to resolve his dilemma. God miraculously and mercifully comes to the rescue. He condescends to sinful, dead man, depraved in all his being through sin, and enlivens him together with Christ. Man does not deserve this. He deserves the opposite because of his sin. But God is merciful in salvation. The resurrection is a stirring confirmation of the grace of God's covenant promise.

In preaching the resurrection, Peter stresses the sovereignty and grace of God's covenant. In Jesus, God comes to fallen man, reveals the supremacy of the divine will, exposes the wickedness of man's sinful nature and fulfils his plan to save man from his sin. The resurrection confirms the truth of God's promise. In plain terms, Peter tells these Jews that they had murdered their Messiah and, in so doing, had tried to thwart the sovereignty and grace of God's promise. But God countered their designs by raising Jesus from the dead, just as he had promised in the Scriptures. Any aspiration David had was merely a pale reflection of this reality.

Resurrection according to Paul

Paul preached the same facts with slightly different emphases at Pisidian Antioch. In proclaiming the resurrection, he highlights the realization of God's gospel, his steadfast love for rebellious man. Recounting Israel's history Paul majors on David, a man after God's own heart, doing everything God wants him to do. From David's descendants God has brought to Israel the Saviour, Jesus, as he promised. In condemning Jesus, the people fulfilled the words of the prophets. But God raised Jesus from the dead and there are living witnesses to that. This is supremely good news. The 'raising up' of Jesus, in his coming, death and resurrection, comprises the gospel. Paul proves the incarnation from Psalm 2:7, the resurrection from Isaiah 55:3 and Psalm 16:10.

'We tell you the good news: What God promised our fathers he has fulfilled for us, their children, by raising up Jesus. As it is written in the second Psalm:

"'You are my Son;
    today I have become your Father."

'The fact that God raised him from the dead, never to decay, is stated in these words:

"'I will give you the holy and sure blessings promised to David."

'So it is stated elsewhere:

"'You will not let your Holy One see decay"'
                                                    (Acts 13:32-35).

This is the *love* of God's covenant. Throughout the revelation of God's covenant in the Bible love is present. The special word for this in Hebrew is *hesed*, 'steadfast love'. *Hesed* is God's faithfulness to his covenant promise. God shows his steadfast love to us, but we can respond with our steadfast love towards God. *Hesed* is a two-way word in this sense. It is different from the Hebrew *hen*, 'grace'. *Hen* can only be used for God's condescending favour to us. We cannot respond to God with *hen* but we can with *hesed*.

People often think of election as cold and forbidding, but it is not presented that way in Scripture. God's choosing is warm and loving. The word for 'choose' in Hebrew is *bachar*. It means 'to set affection on someone or something exclusively'. It is the word for a boy falling in love with a girl, choosing her and prizing her above all others. God's electing grace is like that. It is warm with his *hesed*, his 'steadfast love'. It springs from his *bachar*, his 'choosing grace'. Paul recalls how the resurrection shows God's faithfulness to his loving promise. God's elect in Christ inherit the blessings promised to David. God preserves them from ultimate decay.

Sometimes the 'foreknowledge' of God mentioned in the Bible in this context is misunderstood. It is taken to mean that God predestined those to eternal life because he 'knew beforehand' that they would accept Christ as Saviour. But this is not the meaning of foreknowledge in Scripture, even of the word itself. As a Hebrew expression, foreknowledge means that God related himself intimately, revealed himself plainly, set his affection beforehand intentionally, on the objects of his favour out of his condescending love. Foreknowledge means predestination and predestination arises from unconditional grace. It is the sheer love of God's covenant.

Paul also cites the resurrection as the fulfilment of God's law, his wisdom offered to resolve man's predicament. Try as he might, the stain of sin on man's life was indelibly imprinted. The law of Moses only offered partial hope. Sacrifices, however conscientiously offered, only dealt with infringements of the law from a ceremonial point of view. Unwitting sins were remitted but intentional offences, sins 'with a high hand', remained unforgiven. The guilty conscience was still there. David realized this in his guilt over the Bathsheba affair. Against God only, in one sense, had he sinned. Paul sees the resolution of David's and all mankind's dilemma in the gospel of Christ incarnate, crucified, risen. 'For what the law was powerless to do in that it was weakened by the sinful nature, God did by sending his own Son in the likeness of sinful man to be a sin offering'(Rom. 8:3). Jesus' resurrection proved that God's good news was supremely wise, right and effective. 'Therefore, my brothers, I want you to know that through Jesus the forgiveness of sins is proclaimed to you. Through him everyone who believes is justified from everything you could not be justified from by the law of Moses' (Acts 13:38-39).

> Thou hast fulfilled the law
> And we are justified.
> Ours is the blessing, thine the curse;
> We live for thou hast died.
>
> (Mrs Pennyfather)

This is the *wisdom* of God's covenant. Wisdom in Scripture is not theoretical, but very practical. Bezalel was given expertise or wisdom to do work for the tabernacle. The book of Proverbs personalizes wisdom almost as a prophecy of Christ. Christ is made to his people wisdom from God. His death is not foolishness but wisdom, not a stumbling-block but power. The resurrection of Christ is part of this wisdom. It brings home to us God's saving plan. It confirms that God has done in Christ what the law is powerless to do for man because of sin. There is divine wisdom about God's covenant plan of salvation.

Paul combines the love and wisdom of God's covenant in his assessment of the resurrection. It is the pledge of God's active concern for rebellious man in his flight from God. It is the guarantee of God's provision for fallen man in his dilemma before God. It bursts with life-giving hope to man ensnared by sin and death. David knew the covenant of God securing past, present and future. But this was much greater. Paul proclaims Jesus in his resurrection as the ultimate realization of David's aspiration. This is in every way good news, not only that Jesus had conquered death but that, in this, God's love was assured to sinful man and God's wisdom was available for blinded man. Man could anticipate joy in God's presence and eternal pleasures at his right hand as a forgiven and justified sinner through the gospel of Christ. There is something quite definite and particular in what God does for his people both in the death and resurrection of Christ.

Who moved the stone?

Frank Morison's book on the resurrection *Who Moved the Stone?* has always intrigued me. The author, a young law student living at the beginning of the century, when the historicity of Jesus was under attack, had an awesome admiration for the person of Jesus, but many questions about the validity of the biblical account of Jesus as Christ. He set out to examine the last week of Jesus' life with a view to disproving the resurrection. That book was never written. Instead, Frank Morison was convinced of the reality of the risen Christ, became a Christian, and as a result wrote *Who Moved The Stone?*, a vigorous affirmation of the fact of the resurrection.

The book is ingeniously written. It examines the evidence in the most exciting of ways. It is like reading an Agatha Christie thriller and just as gripping. Witnesses are called to give evidence — the principal fisherman, Peter; the prisoner's brother, James; the man from Tarsus, Paul — and their submissions objectively weighed. The evidence of Peter and Paul is of particular interest.

Peter's volatile and simple character is noted. He is transparently open, frank and earnest; a plain, honest fisherman, the kind of man who is peculiarly susceptible to reason, when the hot rush of some emotion is past. What he said at Pentecost on Jesus' resurrection, Morison regards as clear and definite: 'Moreover, there is a certain primitive quality about the phraseology of his speech which stamps it as belonging to a much earlier stratum of belief than that which the historian actually wrote.'

To Morison, what Peter did *not* say on that occasion was of equal importance with what he did say. Peter omits all reference to the evidence of the women in his Pentecost sermon, not because the women never saw the risen Jesus, but because their evidence was unnecessary. By then, the resurrection was an undisputed fact. 'Thus, whether we consider the recorded speeches in the Acts or even their more significant omissions, we reach the conclusion that the witness of the fisherman Peter to the physical vacancy of the grave is beyond question.'

Paul was so different a character: intellectual, religious, a university man. He comes to the resurrection from an entirely different angle. Morison notes Paul's calm acceptance of this stupendous fact, as compared to Peter's initial incredulity. Above all, he sees Paul's enduring mental conviction as to the truth of the resurrection after his Damascus Road experience. 'When Saul was really convinced that he had seen the risen Jesus the immense and overpowering significance of the empty tomb swept for the first time into his mind. It was as though the great stone itself had crashed into and carried away his last defences. He saw that if the disciples were not deceivers, then they were *right*, right through the whole range and gamut of their claim... He began to understand why Peter was so sure and why everyone connected with this movement was so unaccountably joyous and so immovably convinced.'

The most amazing feature of all about the evidence of both Peter and Paul to the resurrection of Jesus is that it was scripturally orientated. Peter had the testimony of the women, his own and the disciples' experiences of meeting the risen Christ. Paul had his Damascus Road experience. But the nerve-centre of their conviction, the burden of their persuasion, the source of their triumphant proclamation of the resurrection was Scripture. They mention witnesses, but they major on Scripture. Right from the very outset of their preaching and, certainly so far as Paul is concerned, later in his writing, Scripture is the final proof and guarantee of Jesus' rising. God had said it would happen and so it did. Jesus rose, just as he himself had said (Matt. 28:6; Mark 16:6-7; Luke 24:6-8). Christ was crucified and rose again the third day 'according to the Scriptures' (1 Cor. 15:3-4). That was the most amazing feature of all about their evidence. David had prophesied the resurrection in Psalm 16 on the basis of the covenant. But David was dead, buried, entombed and decayed. Jesus fulfilled the covenant promise of Psalm 16 in his death and resurrection. This was an example of the sovereignty, a confirmation of the grace, a realization of the love and a fulfilment of the wisdom of God's covenant — and Jesus, who had died, was now alive for evermore. That was proof beyond all question of contradiction. In the event, both Peter and Paul look to the Scripture, and specifically to Psalm 16, for their proof of Jesus' resurrection. The resurrection was rooted in the covenant plan of God, a plan evident throughout the Old Testament in general, but pointedly relevant, in this instance, to Psalm 16 in particular.

Resurrection according to Hebrews

There is an interesting postscript to the story. Peter and Paul quote Psalm 16 to prove the resurrection as fulfilling God's covenant. The writer to the Hebrews alludes to the resurrection as fulfilling God's covenant too. In his only direct reference to the resurrection, in a concluding benediction to his letter, the author to the Hebrews imprints this truth indelibly on our minds: 'May the God of peace, who through the blood of the eternal covenant brought back from the dead our Lord Jesus, that great Shepherd of the sheep, equip you with everything good for doing his will, and may he work in us what is pleasing to him, through Jesus Christ, to whom be glory for ever and ever. Amen' (Heb. 13:20-21).

The writer to the Hebrews sees the resurrection as a declaration of God's saving intention — regeneration of fallen man. There were plenty of Old Testament indications of this intention. Isaiah recalls a covenant shepherd (Isa. 63:11), Zechariah covenant blood (Zech. 9:11), Jeremiah foretells a new covenant (Jer. 31:31), Ezekiel a covenant of peace (Ezek. 34:25; 37:26). The author combines all these elements in his overview of Jesus' resurrection. The resurrection was specifically to 'equip' his readers with everything good for doing God's will. The word is a graphic description. It speaks of 'reconciling warring factions', or 'repairing broken bones'. God's covenant purpose in regeneration is a work of rectification and restoration, on the vertical axis between God and man, on the horizontal, between man and man and, in individual experience, it promises a mending of broken lives, a healing of sinful creatures. It is not a mere cosmetic exercise of superficial repair, but a work of total renovation.

This is the *regeneration* of God's covenant. This is why we speak of God's grace as irresistible. It is not that sinful man cannot oppose it, for he does. It is rather that there is about God's grace an enlivening, quickening quality which brings death to life and barrenness to fertility. God's grace confers life; it is, in essence, a regenerating force. In that sense, it is irresistible. It sweeps all opposition aside. And the index of this is the power which brought Jesus back from death to life. We are born again to a living hope by the resurrection of Christ from the dead (1 Peter 1:3). This exemplifies the regeneration of God's covenant.

The writer to the Hebrews also sees the resurrection as a determination of God's action, God's initiative in man's salvation. The initiative of God had always been an Old Testament feature of God's covenant. Covenants between men, like David and Jonathan, were human pacts between equals, but God's covenant with man was a divine disposition bestowed by a superior on an inferior for the latter's benefit and well-being. God always took the initiative. As we have already seen, God called Abraham in covenant, confirmed it to Moses, renewed it with David, explained it through Isaiah, predicted it by Jeremiah and completed it in Christ.

Here, too, the writer stresses God's initiative. God not only equips us for doing his will, but does his will in us. The verb for both God's action and ours is exactly the same. As Aquinas put it, 'This

is the will of God that we should will what God wills; for otherwise
we have no good will. But God's will is our good.' This is
remarkable, for there is here a unity of man's will with the will and
work of God. So Paul reminds the Philippians to work out the
salvation which God is already working in them and tells the
Ephesians that they are God's workmanship created in Christ Jesus
for good works (Phil. 2:13; Eph. 2:10).

This is the *divine initiative* of God's covenant. This is the reason
for the perseverance of the saints. It is not so much that we persevere,
though we do, but that God preserves us, doing his will in us, even
causing us to do his will. What a mighty encouragement for the
believer! God's power undergirds not only our justification but our
sanctification. God not only brings us to life but preserves us in that
life. We are born again into an inheritance that can never perish,
spoil or fade, kept in heaven for us. We are shielded by God's power
until the coming of the salvation that is ready to be revealed in the
last time (1 Peter 1:4-5). The inheritance is kept for us and we are
kept for it. There is a double assurance, a perseverance of the saints
from both the manward and Godward side. This is the result of the
divine initiative of God's covenant.

This is evident in the good works to which Christians are
foreordained (Eph. 2:10). The remarkable thing about those of
whom Christ spoke, as having cared for him inasmuch as they
showed kindness to one of the least of his brothers, was that they
were unaware of this goodness. 'When did we do this?' they asked
(Matt. 25:31-46). Such is the perseverance of God's grace that even
unconsciously believers show the fruit of the good works to which
they are foreordained.

The most striking feature of all is that the power which brings this
about is the resurrection. Peter writes that believers are born again
by the resurrection of Christ from the dead and Paul that they are not
only dead and buried with Christ, but risen with him (1 Peter 1:3;
Rom. 6:3-4). The resurrection of Christ not only pledges the
sovereignty and grace of God's covenant and proclaims its love and
wisdom, it also produces the divine initiative and regeneration of the
covenant. The covenant, as exemplified in the resurrection, is not
only sovereignly powerful and warmly attractive but eminently
effective. It really works. It equips us to do God's will, for God does
his will in us.

The Saviour died, but rose again
Triumphant from the grave;
And pleads our cause at God's right hand,
Omnipotent to save.

Who then can e'er divide us more
From Jesus and his love,
Or break the sacred chain that binds
The earth to heaven above?

Let troubles rise, let terrors frown
And days of darkness fall;
Through him all dangers we'll defy,
And more than conquer all.

Nor death nor life, nor earth nor hell,
Nor time's destroying sway,
Can e'er efface us from his heart,
Or make his love decay.

Each future period that will bless
As it has bless'd the past;
He lov'd us from the first of time,
He loves us to the last.

(Scottish Paraphrases)

David's aspirations of eternal life through the covenant in Psalm 16 are fulfilled in Jesus, the risen Lord. What David could never have personally experienced was provided for him by his greater Son: a perfect covenant work, complete and assured in every part — past, present and future. The sovereignty, grace, love and wisdom of God's covenant of salvation are all forecast in the resurrection prophecy of Psalm 16. Peter and Paul make this clear. The writer to the Hebrews underscores the divine initiative and regeneration of this covenant work. The Christ of Psalm 16 is the risen Lord who accomplishes God's saving covenant of grace.

7.
High Priest

Psalm 110 is an oracle about a king who is also a priest. It has its roots in David and God's great promise to him that he would establish his dynasty. But it goes far beyond David and his successors. Indeed, of all the psalms we have examined, it is quite clearly Messianic and points forward to the coming Messiah and Deliverer of God's people.

There is a combination of the offices of kingship and priesthood in the psalm. The central figure is a king-priest, a royal pontiff, a priestly ruler. Both aspects are there, in equal measure, uniting in this one person, neither giving way to the other. This is truly remarkable, for throughout the entire Old Testament these two offices, both divine appointments symbolized by anointing, were sharply distinct and were to be kept that way according to God's revelation in Scripture. Kings who ruled the people in God's name were forbidden to participate in priestly duties. Priests who represented the people before God by officiating at the altar and teaching the law were not to impinge on the regal function. Yet here, in this psalm, the two are fused into one.

The most dramatic feature of all about the psalm, however, is the way the king-priest is presented. The marks of his kingly function are precisely the same as those of his priestly work. Glancing quickly down the song from its description of king to that of priest, we see that deity, sovereignty and eternity are successively ascribed to each office in turn. It is as though we are meant to gather from this strange picture of the king-priest a unified view of the duty of his person and the almighty timelessness of his work. These visuals highlight the message more clearly. We gaze at the figure before us, sharply aware of an impressive unity of two offices which were once quite distinct and separate. The coming Messiah will be a king-priest, divine, sovereign and eternal.

Deity

The origin of the mysterious person of the king-priest is divine. The source of his deity is stressed. This is so with regard to the *kingly* Messiah:

'The Lord says to my Lord:
  "Sit at my right hand
until I make your enemies
  a footstool for your feet"'

(Ps. 110:1).

Whatever of this may refer to David, the name and relationship of the king-priest to God go far beyond that. David could rightly regard himself as favoured by God and could boast of the esteem in which he was held by the people as their lord and master. But his language here exceeds all personal reference. David depicts the covenant God by his unutterable name JAHWEH. Then he addresses his own lord and master as ADONAI, literally 'my Master', another Old Testament title for God. David, privy to the divine conversation between Father and Son, as it were, stands aside and bows before JAHWEH and ADONAI. David is the third party here. Ultimate reference could never be to him. Further, ADONAI is commanded to sit at God's right hand. Whatever blessings from God David had experienced, ascending the divine throne was certainly not one of them. David describes here names and relationships of deity.

Deity also marks the origin of the *priestly* Messiah:

'The Lord has sworn
  and will not change his mind:
"You are a priest for ever,
  in the order of Melchizedek"'

(Ps. 110:4).

Again, it is the name and relationship of the king-priest to God which outstrip all reference to David. Here the matter is even clearer than with the kingly Messiah. Melchizedek's name means, literally, 'King of righteousness'. Yet he is described as a 'priest'. Melchizedek alone combines the kingly and priestly offices. His relationship to God is unique too. His appointment is directly divine. He is established in office by God's oath. Melchizedek, without forebears or descendants, is appointed by God. His ancestry is of no consequence, unlike the necessary qualification for the Levitical priesthood. His appointment is by divine oath, not human ancestry.

David knows this. He recognizes the king-priest Melchizedek to have existed even before the house of Levi. He realizes, from Old Testament Scripture, that Melchizedek is superior to Abraham, for Abraham offers Melchizedek tithes. He sees how God eventually sets the tribe of Levi apart to serve at the altar. David will not make the same mistake as Saul made when he offered sacrifice and was rejected by God for his disobedience. When David speaks of a priest 'for ever in the order of Melchizedek', appointed directly on God's oath, he is clearly not thinking of himself or of his dynasty, but of the king-priest Messiah who is to come.

The deity of both king and priest points forward to the person of Messiah, in whom both kingship and priesthood, humanity and divinity are combined.

Sovereignty

Sovereignty characterizes the nature of the *kingly* Messiah's work:

'The Lord will extend your mighty sceptre from Zion;
    you will rule in the midst of your enemies'

(Ps. 110:2).

David had known immense blessing on his kingship. From the early days of Saul's threats, David had gone on to experience the quiet progress of God extending his power. When Saul had eventually been dethroned, David's power was mightily established. The perimeters of Israel's nationhood had never been as far extended as then. David's writ ran unhindered from the Euphrates in the north to Egypt in the south. Even the civil strife of Absalom's rebellion and the sporadic attacks of Philistine marauders were insufficient to curtail David's sovereignty.

David could well have referred the lyric of his song to his own reign as king. But that would have been insufficient. David knew the ultimate extension of the sceptre from Zion was not geographically conditioned. He realized that the authority he exercised, even at the height of his power and over his own enemies, was not the complete fulfilment of these words. This total sovereignty was on a world, not a local scale. It was absolute, not conditional. It awaited further consummation.

Sovereignty was also of the nature of the *priestly* Messiah's work:

'The Lord is at your right hand;
  he will crush kings on the day of his wrath.
He will judge nations, heaping up the dead
  and crushing the rulers of the whole earth'

(Ps. 110:5-6).

The priestly Melchizedek discloses the full extent of Messiah's sovereignty. Here again, the forecast of events is less applicable to David even than in the case of the kingly Messiah. It is not simply kings who are crushed but nations who are judged. This is not limited to the surrounding confederacies and competing powers, but a defeat of the rulers of the whole earth. The triumph is on a cosmic scale.

The amazing feature about it, too, is that it is accomplished not primarily by kingly but by priestly function. Judgement, in terms both of assessing infringements of the law and meting out punishment, was the priest's particular preserve in teaching the Torah. World dominion is accomplished here by this process, for behind the sovereignty lies the sworn oath of God. Such cosmic proportions from such judicial process go far beyond any view of David's earthly kingship. The coming king-priest alone would secure this.

Eternity

Eternity also marks the quality of the *kingly* Messiah's work:

'Your troops will be willing
  on your day of battle.

Arrayed in holy majesty,
    from the womb of the dawn
    you will receive the dew of your youth'

(Ps. 110:3).

David knew much about faithful troops and willing soldiers. His mighty men were faithful and willing, just as were the fighting men under them. His three commanders-in-chief showed such faithfulness when they risked life and limb during the heat of battle to bring their master a drink from his favourite well at Bethlehem. But the troops of the king-priest are superior. There is an eternal dimension to their allegiance. They are arrayed 'in holy majesty'. 'Splendour of holiness' belongs to these soldiers. This same phrase is used in Psalm 29:2 to describe the divine glory: 'Worship the Lord in the splendour of his holiness.' Eternity itself, as an other-worldly quality, characterizes this army. It is conferred upon them by the divine king-priest. David could never give this to his troops.

Nor could David create the endless host of warriors born into Messiah's army. He may often have gazed at the numberless beads of dew on the grass around him as he woke in the crispness of the dawn during his flights from Saul and thought of the miracle of this freshness after the dry dust of the previous evening. But what is he viewing here? It is a myriad of endlessly youthful troops, miraculously faithful and fresh in their allegiance to their master. This is a picture of regeneration in the Old Testament. No human king could ever host an army of that nature or on that scale.

Eternity was also of the quality of the *priestly* Messiah's activity:

'He will drink from a brook beside the way;
    therefore he will lift up his head'

(Ps. 110:7).

David would have recalled his own gasping thirst on many occasions, but especially during that final Philistine onslaught when he longed for a drink from the well of Bethlehem. The king-priest would never be frantically parched like that. Completely in control of both himself and the situation, with an eternal freshness in his character, he would revive himself from the brook and continue in hot pursuit. A constant newness would mark his activity, a continual brightness his prospect. Neither David, nor any other man, could aspire to this.

The king-priest

Deity, sovereignty and eternity mark the work of the Messiah, who is both king and priest. What does this impressive, unified view of the king-priest Messiah teach? Why is there this startling similarity of deity, sovereignty and eternity in the king who is priest and the priest who is king? Into what unfolding sequence of Scripture about the Messiah does Psalm 110 fit?

God had early established the principle of a king-priest figure in Melchizedek. Abraham, returning from battle, meets Melchizedek, King of Salem and priest of the Most High God, in the region of Jerusalem, when it was little more than a pagan encampment. Melchizedek brings bread and wine to Abraham and blesses him in the name of God Most High. Abraham responds by offering to Melchizedek tithes of all his possessions (Gen. 14:18-20).

God continues by teaching the separation of kingship and priesthood in the clearest terms to his people. From the descendants of Abraham come the tribe of Levi, who alone are responsible among God's people for priesthood and receive tithes from the people to support them in their work (Lev. 7:28 - 9:23; Num. 3; 4). Any usurpation of these duties on the part of others brings from God the severest censure. Saul, who offered sacrifice, is rejected by God from kingship for his disobedience (1 Sam. 13:8-14). Uzziah, a later king of Judah, who acted in the same way, was smitten by God with leprosy because of his sin (2 Chron. 26:16-21). Clearly, the offices of king and priest are distinct and are to remain so.

God ultimately promises a coming king-priest for his people. David, though established in Jerusalem, never combined the priestly office with his kingship. Nor had he any intention that his successors should do so. Zadok the priest, together with his family, which was quite distinct from the Davidic line, exercised the chief priesthood in the Jerusalem temple during the period of monarchy (1 Chron. 29:22). Zechariah later predicts kingly and priestly functions of the Messiah for the future: 'Tell him this is what the Lord Almighty says: "Here is the man whose name is the Branch, and he will branch out from his place and build the temple of the Lord. It is he who will build the temple of the Lord, and he will be clothed with majesty and will sit and rule on his throne. And he will be a priest on his throne. And there will be harmony between the two"' (Zech. 6:12-13). Even in Zechariah's day the offices remained distinct. The 'two anointed ones' were Zerubbabel the king and Joshua the priest. The fusion of these offices was still future.

It is into this sequence that the Messiah of Psalm 110 fits. He comes as king-priest, divine, sovereign and eternal, both in his person and work, to fulfil God's gracious and glorious purpose for his people:

> 'The Lord says to my Lord:
>   "Sit at my right hand
> until I make your enemies
>   a footstool for your feet."
> The Lord will extend your mighty sceptre from Zion;
>   you will rule in the midst of your enemies.
> Your troops will be willing
>   on your day of battle.
> Arrayed in holy majesty,
>   from the womb of the dawn
>   you will receive the dew of your youth.
> The Lord has sworn
>   and will not change his mind:
> "You are a priest for ever,
>   in the order of Melchizedek."
> The Lord is at your right hand;
>   he will crush kings on the day of his wrath.
> He will judge nations, heaping up the dead
>   and crushing the rulers of the whole earth.
> He will drink from a brook beside the way;
>   therefore he will lift up his head'

(Ps. 110).

Christ fulfils the glorious prophecy of Psalm 110. He combines the offices of king and priest. A host of New Testament witnesses quote this psalm and teach this truth — Jesus, Peter, Paul, the writer to the Hebrews and John. All testify to the kingly and priestly attributes of the Messiah. The remarkable thing about two of these witnesses, Jesus and the writer to the Hebrews, is that they do this in a strikingly similar manner. The context, reasoning and result of their testimonies combine to validate Jesus as king-priest, both in his person and work, on precisely the same lines. The one emphasizes kingship, the other priesthood. Together they offer incontrovertible proof that, as far as the New Testament is concerned, Psalm 110 is

Messianic. Jesus is the kingly and priestly Messiah. He fulfils the prediction perfectly.

Vindication

Jesus teaches that he himself, as *kingly* Messiah, brings vindication to his cause. As king-priest, he accomplishes completely all his Father had given him to do. There can be no argument against this, no gainsaying of it. He silences all opposition, affirms the wisdom of God's plan and celebrates the triumph of God's purpose. God's deity, sovereignty and eternity are evident in Jesus the King-Priest.

The context of Jesus' teaching anticipates this. It was the last fateful week of Jesus' troubled life. His actions and words took on a judgemental note. The end was drawing near. He enters Jerusalem, a lowly king, riding in state on a donkey. He cleanses the temple, a furious priest, ridding the house of Levi of impurity. He curses the fig-tree, in an acted parable, visiting God's wrath on a reluctant people. He responds to a barrage of questions with clarity and sharpness — concerning his own authority, taxation by Caesar, marriage after death. He affirms the legitimacy of his kingdom, rejected by men but established by God. He emphasizes the supremacy of the greatest commandment, love to God and to one's neighbour, over against religious observance. But all of Jesus' actions and words are merely a prelude to his ultimate claim, that he is Christ, the son of David. That above all, validates his authority and vindicates his claim. That is the climax. That is when Jesus quotes Psalm 110:

'While the Pharisees were gathered together, Jesus asked them, "What do you think about the Christ? Whose son is he?"

'"The son of David," they replied.

'He said to them, "How is it then that David, speaking by the Spirit, calls him 'Lord'? For he says,

'"'The Lord said to my Lord:
"Sit at my right hand
until I put your enemies
under your feet."'

"'If then David calls him 'Lord', how can he be his son?'"
(Matt. 22:41-45).

The reasoning behind Jesus' teaching authenticates his person as
kingly Messiah. Jesus settles the matter of the authorship and the
Messianic nature of the psalm in one short comment. He questions
his questioners at the end of the debate. More than that, Jesus asserts
that 'David's Lord' is Messiah even though he is David's son. The
priest of Psalm 110 is the king of Psalm 2. Jesus, in fact, implies that
he himself is both son of David and David's Lord, the kingly and
priestly Messiah in one person.

The issue of authority lay behind all this questioning of Jesus'
actions and teaching, and Jesus knew it. Who was he to enter
Jerusalem riding on a donkey, as Zechariah had foretold? Who was
he to cleanse the temple in terms of Malachi's oracle? Who was he
to even hint at being the 'cornerstone' of David's predictions? John
the Baptist's authority the Pharisees did not dare to dispute, for he
was 'Elijah', the great forerunner of the Messiah, and the people
believed that. Jesus of Nazareth's claim they now must consider, for
he claimed to be the 'son of David'. That was why Jesus quoted the
psalm, questioned them about it and made it the basis of his claim,
albeit implicitly, to the office of king-priest, the son of David, the
kingly Messiah of Israel.

The result of Jesus' teaching validates his work as kingly
Messiah. It was tremendously effective, for it silenced all opposition. It closed the debate. It left his opponents without a word to
say. In fact, it left them with a question to answer. It shifted the
emphasis of discussion to its proper centre and focus. It was not only
proof of Jesus' claim to the person of the kingly Messiah; it
confirmed the activity of his work in that office too. He rules
supreme over his enemies. He, the Messiah, is at the right hand of
God; his enemies are under his feet. 'No one could say a word in
reply, and from that day on no one dared to ask him any more
questions' (Matt. 22:46).

Matthew's comment says it all. Mark and Luke make the same
observation at a slightly different place. They locate it immediately
after Jesus' successful answer to the lawyer's question about the
greatest commandment and immediately before Jesus' quotation
from Psalm 110. For Mark and Luke, the trend of the debate is very
clear. Jesus has triumphed over his questioners even at this early

point. Matthew reserves his comment until after Jesus' challenging question. But all three Gospel writers are saying the same thing with a slightly different emphasis. They concur in recognizing Jesus' victory. He has acted out his Messianic claims publicly and effectively taught them by response and comment. Jesus' quotation from Psalm 110, arising from his challenge to his questioners, marks the triumphant climax to his actions and words. It is demonstrably clear that he is the king-priest Messiah both in deed and word, in person and work. In fact, it has been clear all along. This final note tops it all! There is nothing more to say.

All the other witnesses agree, too. For Peter, the Messiah of Psalm 110 is both Lord and Christ; for Stephen, his eternal hope; for Paul, his risen, ruling, ascended and interceding Lord; for the writer to the Hebrews, a perfect priest and a finished sacrifice; for John on Patmos, a triumphant victor. The king-priest brings total vindication to his cause. There is no room for further discussion. He is at God's right hand; his enemies are under his feet.

A number of years ago, I was assistant minister in a city church. We were preparing for our Youth Service. We had picked our praise items, prepared our youth choir, prayed for the whole project but something was still on my mind. The young people wanted a 'talk-back' session after the service. It was the 'in' thing in those days. We must not stand six feet above contradiction in our lofty pulpits but discuss our assertions with our hearers. In one sense, it was fair enough; in another quite a fearful prospect.

With some unease, I prepared the word, asking God to help with every expression. The service seemed to go well. We went over to the church hall for coffee and 'talk-back'. It was a delight to see how many adults joined us. It was that kind of congregation. They knew what biblical family fellowship meant. After supper, the discussion started. The questions were reasonable, certainly not divisive. Indeed, as time passed, they became interesting, exciting even. Asked to give some detail about a person coming to faith, I tried to be as clear and as down-to-earth as possible.

Then it happened. A teenage girl, whom I knew to have been interested, stood to her feet and said unashamedly, publicly and unemotionally that if that was what it meant to recognize one's sin and to come in repentance and faith to the Saviour, she was near that point. I staggered in bewilderment but praised God in my heart. I thought of the lawyer and his question to Jesus about the greatest commandment. Above all, I thought of Jesus' words: 'You are not far from the kingdom of God' (Mark 12:34). A silence dropped on the 'talk-back'. There may have been more questions, I cannot rightly remember, but they were of little consequence. God had taken complete control. What could have been arid, divisive debate became meaningful spiritual discussion. The kingly Messiah, by his Spirit through the Word, was vindicating his cause, silencing opposition and causing delightful interest. His deity, sovereignty and eternity were validated before us. He was sitting at God's right hand, his enemies under his feet, and we were knowing something of the power of a risen, ascended, exalted, interceding King-Priest at work that evening. Christ's cause was vindicated among us. There was nothing more to say. I never forgot that service and I never will. We need to recover the centrality of the King-Priest's sovereignty in all our evangelistic efforts.

> Jesus, the Saviour, reigns,
> The God of truth and love;
> When he had purged our stains,
> He took his seat above:
> Lift up your heart, lift up your voice;
> Rejoice, again I say, 'Rejoice'.
>
> He sits at God's right hand
> Till all his foes submit,
> And bow to his command,
> And fall beneath his feet:
> Lift up your heart, lift up your voice
> Rejoice; again I say, 'Rejoice'.
>
> (Charles Wesley).

Victory

The writer to the Hebrews, in presenting Jesus as the *priestly* Messiah of Psalm 110, shows how he gives victory to his people. The entire letter to the Hebrews is about Jesus' priesthood. Jesus is the perfect priest, who offers a perfect sacrifice for his people. His priesthood is perfect, for he is both divine and human. His sacrifice is perfect too. It is offered in the proper way, not an animal but a self-sacrifice. It is presented in the proper place, before God rather than in the temple. It is given within a proper time-scale, 'once for all', with finality, not continually as with Old Testament sacrifices.

The author of Hebrews fits the Melchizedek theme from Psalm 110 into this structure. The remarkable thing is the similarity in format with the teaching of Jesus. The context, reasoning and results in the instruction given in his letter have precisely the same implications as Jesus' quotation of Psalm 110. The deity, sovereignty and eternity of Christ's person and work are clear. Just as Jesus, from Psalm 110, stressed the vindication he himself brings to his cause as a *kingly* Messiah, so the writer of Hebrews underscores the victory Christ gives to his people as a *priestly* Messiah. The similarity of presentation is gripping and helpful.

The context of this teaching in the letter to the Hebrews anticipates the victory Christ gives his people. What had happened to the offices of kingship and priesthood since the close of the Old Testament? Were there any significant developments of these during the period between the Old and New Testaments? Indeed there were. Judas ben Matthias, a Jewish hero, known by the Greek surname Maccabees, established a dynasty in Palestine under the family name Hasmon, the Hasmonæans. He and his successors rebelled against the heirs of the Greek, Alexander the Great, the Ptolemys of Egypt and the Seleucids of Syria. From the time of Judas' brother Jonathan Maccabæus onwards, the chief priesthood and chief civil power in Israel were combined in one person. The Hasmonæans had nothing to do with Melchizedek. For them, it was an ideal political ploy. Nevertheless, strongly pious groups in Judaism, like the Pharisees, descendants of the Hasidim who had supported the Hasmonæans, and the community of Qumran, a priestly sect living in the region of the Dead Sea, strongly disapproved of this fusion of kingly and priestly power. Antigonus, the last of the Hasmonæan high-priestly kings, was executed in 37 B.C., and the pro-Roman Herod the Great began a new era. The combination of kingship and priesthood had failed under the Hasmonæans. When Jesus was born, Israel still awaited the king-priest of Psalm 110. The writer to the Hebrews affirms clearly that Jesus is this very king-priest. Where the Hasmonæan dynasty of the Maccabeans failed, Jesus, the lion of the tribe of Judah, succeeds. That is the background against which the author to the Hebrews writes of Jesus, 'a high-priest of the order of Melchizedek':

'He of whom these things are said belonged to a different tribe, and no one from that tribe has ever served at the altar. For it is clear that our Lord descended from Judah, and in regard to that tribe Moses said nothing about priests. And what we have said is even more clear if another priest like Melchizedek appears, one who has become a priest not on the basis of a regulation as to his ancestry but on the basis of the power of an indestructible life. For it is declared:

"You are a priest for ever,
in the order of Melchizedek"'
                                               (Heb. 7:13-17).

The reasoning of the writer to the Hebrews confirms the victory of Christ's person as priestly Messiah. Two things are clear to the writer. Firstly, Jesus is descended not from the tribe of Levi but from that of Judah, of which the law says nothing in regard to priestly function. Secondly, Jesus is a priest of the order of Melchizedek, not of Levi, appointed not on the basis of human ancestry, but on the power of an eternal life. But what had the writer said about Melchizedek that makes him sure that Jesus belongs to that order of priesthood?

Firstly, he had said that the order is *superior*: Melchizedek, King of Salem and priest of God Most High, blesses Abraham returning from battle. Abraham offers tithes. Blessing is the prerogative of the superior, giving tithes the obligation of the inferior. In fact, the writer argues, the tribe of Levi, not yet born, offer tithes through Abraham their ancestor and thus declare their inferior obligation to Melchizedek (Heb. 7:1-10).

Secondly, he had said that Melchizedek's order is *eternal*: 'Without father or mother, without genealogy, without beginning of days or end of life, like the Son of God he remains a priest for ever' (Heb. 7:3).

The writer further reasons that Jesus fits the qualifications of Melchizedek's order perfectly. Jesus does not come from Levi and thus is barred from human priesthood, but he comes from Judah and so is plainly in the line of kingship. However, Jesus is superior because he is the eternal Son of God, appointed to his priesthood and kingship not in terms of human ancestry but on the basis of an indestructible life. Jesus is clearly not of Levi's order, but of

Melchizedek's. Jesus, the lion of the tribe of Judah, not Levi nor Maccabæus nor any other, is Melchizedek. The prophecy of Psalm 110 is ultimately fulfilled in Jesus of Nazareth, the priestly Messiah.

The results of the writer to the Hebrews' reasoning stress the victory which Christ gains for his people through his work as priestly Messiah:

'The former regulation is set aside because it was weak and useless (for the law made nothing perfect), and a better hope is introduced, by which we draw near to God.

'And it was not without an oath! Others became priests without any oath, but he became a priest with an oath when God said to him:

'"The Lord has sworn
   and will not change his mind:
'You are a priest for ever.'"

'Because of this oath, Jesus has become the guarantee of a better covenant'

(Heb. 7:18-22).

Not only the person of Christ as priestly Messiah is superior and eternal, his work is too. The writer constantly stresses the weakness of the Levitical priesthood. It was weak because it was fallible in the hands of fallen men. It was weak because it was finite, bounded by the lifetime of dying men. This had grave implications for its entire structure. The fallen, finite priests produced a flawed, imperfect system. So a change is necessary: 'For when there is a change of the priesthood, there must also be a change of the law,' the writer claimed (Heb. 7:12).

What was needed was an infallible, infinite priest, a sinless and eternal Messiah. But here is the glory of the situation: Jesus exactly fits those qualifications and so the entire order he introduces, as priest, is not marginally but radically different. He interposes a 'better covenant'.

Furthermore, the source of this new system is related to Jesus' person as priest. God's oath is the basis of his appointment. This was not so in the case of the Levitical priesthood. In this sense, in terms of his appointment, Jesus stands in the order of Abraham and David rather than that of Levi. Covenant, rather than law, is the basis of Jesus' priesthood. Thus the victory Jesus, as priest, bestows on his people is by covenant rather than by law. The writer emphasizes this with three striking word-pictures.

First, Jesus becomes *guarantor* of this better system: 'Because of this oath Jesus has become the guarantee of a better covenant' (Heb. 7:22). This gives a warm, personal note to the victory. The word for 'guarantee', used only here in the New Testament, was common in legal and promissory documents of the day. Here, it is personalized in Jesus the Priest. He is guarantor of our salvation. He personally underwrites our redemption.

Secondly, Jesus grants faith as an *anchor* of the soul, firm and sure: 'God did this so that by two unchangeable things in which it is impossible for God to lie, we who have fled to take hold of the hope offered to us may be greatly encouraged. We have this hope as an anchor for the soul, firm and secure. It enters the inner sanctuary behind the curtain, where Jesus, who went before us, has entered on our behalf. He has become a high priest for ever, in the order of Melchizedek' (Heb. 6:18-20). This adds a dimension of certainty to the victory. Our faith in Christ penetrates the curtain into the holy of holies, where God has promised both to cleanse from sin and to communicate with his people.

Thirdly, Jesus is *mediator* of a new covenant: 'For this reason Christ is the mediator of a new covenant, that those who are called may receive the promised eternal inheritance — now that he has died as a ransom to set them free from the sins committed under the first covenant' (Heb. 9:15). This introduces a qualitative newness to the victory. By calling this covenant 'new', God has made the first one obsolete, and what is obsolete and ageing will soon disappear (Heb. 8:13). Jesus is the mediator of a new covenant. His sprinkled blood speaks a better word than that of Abel (Heb. 12:24). The whole situation is entirely new. The blood of Abel called down divine judgement. The blood of Christ bestows divine forgiveness. The Mosaic covenant was fragile and breakable, not because of God's nature but on account of man's sin. The 'new covenant' is firm and secure, written on our hearts as promised to Abraham, predicted by Jeremiah and ratified in Jesus the Messiah. Covenant grace, not legal observance, is the essence of the priestly Messiah's victory for his people.

Other New Testament witnesses attest this truth. John claims that the law came by Moses but grace and truth through Jesus Christ, the living Word (John 1:17). Paul writes that the law can never set aside the covenant previously established by God and ratified in Christ (Gal. 3:17). Peter boasts an inner cleansing of conscience rather than outward ceremonial washing through the resurrected, ascended Christ who sits at God's right hand (1 Peter 3:21-22).

Christ as high priest gives many blessings to his people. He is their source of sympathy in times of need, their means of strength throughout life's journey and their sacrificial substitute on the cross, as both priest and victim. In these, Christ's divine and human attributes blend, his person and work combine. Here, the author to the Hebrews stresses the stability Christ grants to his people.

The victory, above all, brings assurance of salvation. We can have both faith and assurance of faith. We can not only know him, but also know that we know him. We can have this sureness for he is our guarantor. Our faith is anchored through him in God. We are heirs of a new covenant.

My friend had been a Christian for a number of years. A clear-cut conversion experience in her teens had led to an open Christian profession as a girl. In the course of time, she served her Lord in her home as a wife and mother and used her gifts of song effectively for her Saviour in the fellowship of the church and elsewhere. She had little doubt about being a Christian.

I remember, though, how she told me of the effect a sermon on John 15:16 had on her: 'You did not choose me, but I chose you to go and bear fruit — fruit that will last.' It was quite traumatic. For the first time she began to see the eternal dimension of her salvation. Prior to that, she had thought in terms of her decision for Christ her Saviour. That and that alone was the essence of her conversion. Now she recognized how God had been working in her life even in those years before she became a Christian. She began to take seriously, and to understand, what she read in Scripture about being 'chosen in Christ before the foundation of the world'. Later, when she heard faith expounded as the gift of God, the result, not the cause of her new nature, this simply confirmed the truth to her.

This added a whole new dimension to her Christian experience. It rooted her faith much more deeply in God rather than in her own self-will. It amazed her, in a new way, to think of God's grace and favour to her. It gave her an assurance and victory, not humanly generated but divinely granted. It stabilized her entire Christian experience and made her love for Christ, God and the Scriptures even greater. She had discovered the victory the priestly Messiah gives and it was gradually widening the scope of her Christian life. Her Saviour was her guarantor. Her faith was anchored through him in God. She was heir of a new covenant, and she knew it. It was a delightful discovery. And in all this, it did not trivialize but rather stressed the responsibility of her decision for Christ, the necessity of her personal act of repentance and faith, which she had made years before.

The *Westminster Confession* traces out the difficulties of the experience of this assurance of salvation with clarity and helpfulness:

'This certainty is not a bare conjectural and probable persuasion, grounded upon a fallible hope; but an infallible assurance of faith, founded upon the divine truth of the promises of salvation, the inward evidence of those graces unto which these promises are made, the testimony of the Spirit of adoption witnessing with our spirits that we are the children of God: which Spirit is the earnest of our inheritance, whereby we are sealed to the day of redemption.

'This infallible assurance doth not so belong to the essence of faith, but that a true believer may wait long, and conflict with many difficulties, before he be partaker of it: yet, being enabled by the Spirit to know the things which are freely given him of God, he may, without extraordinary revelation, in the right use of ordinary means, attain thereunto. And therefore it is the duty of every one to give all diligence to make his calling and election sure; that thereby his heart may be enlarged in peace and joy in the Holy Ghost, in love and thankfulness to God, and in strength and cheerfulness in the duties of obedience, the proper fruits of this assurance: so far is it from inclining men to looseness'

(*Westminster Confession,* XVIII, 2,3).

Where high the heavenly temple stands,
The house of God not made with hands,
A great High Priest our nature wears
The guardian of mankind appears.

He who for men their surety stood,
And poured on earth his precious blood,
Pursues in heaven his mighty plan,
The Saviour and the friend of man.

(Scottish Paraphrases)

Psalm 110 reaches its glorious fulfilment in Jesus Christ, the king-priest after the order of Melchizedek. His deity, sovereignty and eternity are in full view. As *kingly* Messiah, his cause is totally vindicated. As *priestly* Messiah, he offers his people the victory of an assured salvation.

What throughout the years of revelation remained separate and distinct, what man's ingenuity could never bring about in the course of human history is now combined in Jesus, the king-priest, who brings to his own cause infinite glory and to his people's eternal comfort: Jesus Christ, a high priest for ever in the order of Melchizedek. Jesus is the king-priest of Psalm 110.

8.
Spiritual Temple

Psalm 118 is a processional psalm. It was used at the major Jewish feasts of the Passover, Pentecost and Tabernacles. It was the last of a group known as the Egyptian Hallel Psalms, because they were composed in praise of God for the exodus from Egypt. There is a sense of occasion about it. The procession makes its way through the narrow streets of Jerusalem, chanting in mournful, yet joyful, theme through the gates, to the temple and eventually to the altar to offer sacrifice to Jehovah. Psalm 118 is the song accompanying this imposing religious procession.

It is also a psalm about the temple. The gates, the building stones and the altar are all in the song. They are the visual effects alongside the vocal expression. There is a sense of presence about the psalm, too — not just the impressiveness of the temple of God but, far more importantly, the significance of the God of the temple, the God who promised to meet with his people between the cherubim above the cover of the ark of the covenant in the inner shrine of the temple. All the fitments and furnishings of both tabernacle and temple come alive in the song and anticipate the God who ultimately presented himself to mankind in the Messiah.

David may well have written the psalm. True, he did not build the temple, but it was always on his mind. He gathered the materials in preparation for it, drew up the plans and left precise instructions for his son Solomon to do the work. It pained David that he and his people dwelt in houses but God lived in a tent. He longed for the day when that would be put right. The materials, the plans and, since it was within his competence, the worship would at least be to hand for his dream to come true and for his God to be truly magnified. That would be done with a sense of occasion and of presence.

The gates

Psalm 118 reflects these longings. God is worthy of praise. He is Israel's helper and refuge. David's enemies disintegrated like swarming bees flying away and like burnt-out thorn branches. David looked around and his foes were gone. God had done this for him. The sight of the tabernacle doors, soon to be replaced by the temple gates, recalled this. As the procession reached the gates, that was evident. Those gates were a surety of God's *protection* to David:

'Our feet are standing
   in your gates, O Jerusalem.
Jerusalem is built like a city
   that is closely compacted together'

(Ps. 122:2-3).

The gates were also the vehicle for God's *praise*.

'Enter his gates with thanksgiving
   and his courts with praise'

(Ps. 100:4).

They were the symbol of God's *presence*. The King of Israel's armies passed through them:

'Lift up your heads, O you gates;
   be lifted up, you ancient doors,
that the King of glory may come in'

(Ps. 24:7,9).

In Psalm 118 not only the king but his righteous subjects pass through the gates. They are 'gates of righteousness' through which only the righteous might enter. They are God's gates, the gates of the God of salvation, as though only through them could the righteous become righteous and so gain entrance. The clean hands and pure heart needed for admittance to God's presence come only through the gates (Ps. 15). The gates, in fact, represented God, 'This is the gate of the Lord,' sang David.

'Open for me the gates of righteousness;
    I will enter and give thanks to the Lord.
This is the gate of the Lord
    through which the righteous may enter.
I will give you thanks, for you answered me;
    you have become my salvation'

(Ps. 118:19-21).

The gates were the agency of God's *salvation.*

The temple

As the gates opened, they disclosed the magnificence of the temple itself. The procession halted and exalted thoughts came to mind. For David, these centred on the building stones and, above all, the cornerstone, which would take the full weight of the structure. The cornerstone would be the epitome of all the temple stood for. Choosing that particular stone, amid all the materials used, was an awesome responsibility over which even master masons would disagree. It was so like his own life and experience of God, David thought — the early troubled days of Saul's enmity, the later difficulties of Absalom's rebellion. David was like a stone disputed over by human builders, but chosen by God and established. His reign and dynasty proved the worth of God's covenant promise of stability.

The strangeness of that disputed stone, chosen by God but rejected by man, repeated itself like a continuing prophecy through Israel's history. In a later generation Isaiah predicted the Messiah as God's cornerstone (Isa. 8:14; 28:16-17). Zechariah encouraged King Zerubbabel with the same promise amid his distresses (Zech. 4:6-10). When the second temple was built and its magnificence proved to be so inferior to Solomon's building that the people had mixed feelings even at its dedication, Haggai warned against superficial judgements in terms of outward splendour and promised King Zerubbabel that God would cause his glory to appear in that very place (Hag. 2:1-9). Even in his own day, David was assured of the divine sovereignty in this stability: 'The Lord has done this and it is marvellous in our eyes.'

> 'The stone the builders rejected
>   has become the capstone;
> the Lord has done this,
>   and it is marvellous in our eyes.
> This is the day the Lord has made;
>   let us rejoice and be glad in it'
>
> (Ps. 118:22-24).

The gates and the cornerstone marked significant points in the progress of the procession. It was all very meaningful to David.

The altar

The offering of sacrifice marked the end of the procession. That was the third feature that gripped David's mind. A profound silence marked that event. As the procession moved to the altar, they hailed the royal leader. 'Blessed is he who comes in the name of the Lord. From the house of the Lord we bless you,' they sang responsively. Then there was silence. The horns were subdued, the clash of the tambourines ceased, the chords of the lyres trailed off into stillness, the singing ended. Only the distant braying and bleating of sacrificial victims was heard. The chosen sacrifice was tied to the altar and the final act of sacrifice began. A thank offering on the altar was the apex of their praise and devotion to God. A sense of climax, finality and anticipation filled the silence.

Why this end to the procession? What meaning lay behind this pregnant silence? David knew it well. The requirement of God's law was there: without the shedding of blood there could be no remission of sins. The practice of David's religion was there: sacrifice — morning, evening, weekly, monthly, annually. The experience of his life was there: the Bathsheba affair, the sleepless nights, the guilty conscience, Nathan's words. But it raised questions in his mind. Was this enough? Was a deeper oblation not necessary? Was not a greater sacrifice required, to which all this pointed? A sense of finality mingled with anticipation marked the climax:

'Against you, you only, have I sinned
    and done what is evil in your sight.
Cleanse me with hyssop, and I shall be clean;
    wash me, and I shall be whiter than snow'

(Ps. 51:4,7).

A living temple

The gates, the cornerstone, the sacrifice were all significant. They were the focal points of the procession. They spelled out the meaning of the song. More than that, they pointed forward inevitably to the coming of the Messiah. The song was ultimately about the Messiah and the effectiveness of his sacrifice. 'The Lord is God, and he has made his light shine upon us,' concluded David.

'O Lord save us;
    O Lord, grant us success.
Blessed is he who comes in the name of the Lord.
    From the house of the Lord we bless you.
The Lord is God,
    and he has made his light shine upon us.
With boughs in hand, join in the festal procession
    up to the horns of the altar.
You are my God, and I will give thanks;
    you are my God, and I will exalt you.
Give thanks to the Lord, for he is good;
    his love endures for ever'

(Ps. 118:25-29).

Psalm 118 is not only a processional psalm about the temple, it is a messianic psalm. That is so particularly with regard to the latter half of the song. It verges on prophecy. It points invariably forward. It anticipates greater things to come. That is how Calvin sees the psalm : 'Let us remember that it was the design of the Spirit, under the figure of this temporal kingdom to describe the eternal and spiritual kingdom of God's Son, even as David represented his person.' The New Testament use of this psalm confirms Calvin's judgement. All Scripture is ultimately about Christ.

The door

David's thoughts about the temple gates are fulfilled in Jesus, the *door* of the sheepfold. The fulfilment is there, but the New Testament alludes to the thought of Psalm 118 rather than directly quoting its words. At first sight, it is not obvious that when Jesus says, 'I am the gate' (John 10:9) this is related to Psalm 118:19-20:

'Open for me the gates of righteousness;
    I will enter and give thanks to the Lord.
This is the gate of the Lord
    through which the righteous may enter.'

It is more of an illustration or legitimate association of ideas than that the gates are actually a type of Christ. But the more we probe Jesus' teaching on the Shepherd and his flock, the clearer the association becomes. It proves a valuable and helpful illustration.

The scene is somewhat different in the New Testament, though, from that we have just described. In the psalm, it is the procession entering the gates into the temple. In the gospel, it is the sheep coming through the door into the sheep-pen. A wide field enclosure provided safe haven for the various flocks during the night. The individual shepherds returned in the morning for their flocks. Often, the sheep would recognize their master's voice, prick up their ears and move to the gate. The gate-man would only open the enclosure when he was assured of the shepherd's identity. In the story, Jesus is both shepherd and door. He is the genuine pastor of the flock as well as the means of access for the sheep to the safety of the fold.

While the scene is different, the moral of the story is the same. Whatever David's temple gates afforded the people of God in the way of God's protection, praise and presence, Jesus the door provides it to an unbelievably greater degree. Whatever entrance David's gates gave in shadowy form to these blessings, Jesus confers in unclouded reality. However David may have conceived of the temple gate as a picture of the Lord of salvation through whom alone the righteous could enter, Jesus affirms that truth of his own person in words beyond all possibility of either doubt or question. David said, 'This is the gate of the Lord' (Ps. 118:20). Jesus said, 'I tell you the truth, I am the gate for the sheep' (John 10:7). Jesus stressed, too, the exclusive nature of himself as the door: the man who enters the pen in any way other than by the door is a thief and robber. Jesus *is* the door. Whoever enters through him will be saved. All who came before him were thieves and robbers; the sheep did not recognize them (John 10:1-10). Jesus is the way, the truth and the life; no one comes to the Father except through him (John 14:6). Jesus makes these claims with incredible solemnity in statements where he puts himself on a par with God, the great I AM of Old Testament revelation. Could there be any more impressive fulfilment than this?

The *exclusiveness* of Jesus as door must grip our attention afresh. Neither the amassing of good works nor attempts at self-reformation nor conscientious observance of religious ordinances gains entry to the kingdom. This access is only through Jesus the door. He affirms this of his own person in an unprecedented claim to divine authority. That is the measure both of the seriousness and veracity of his claim. All we know of God the Father becomes visible in Jesus the Son. Our way of coming to the Father is through him alone. This is the unique and urgent claim of Jesus' saviourhood. We must come through Christ the Saviour alone to God the Father in order to be saved from sin. Jesus is not one way among a variety of avenues offered by the world's religions of coming to God. He is the only way, the exclusive gate into the kingdom.

Jesus is not only an exclusive but also an *effective* door: Jesus *is* the door. Whoever enters through him will be saved. He will come in and go out and find pasture. The thief comes only to kill, steal and destroy. Jesus has come that they might have life and have it to the full (John 10:9-10). The picture is an exciting one. The shepherd not only brings the sheep to the pen for the night but fetches them in the morning. They pass freely through, out to the expansive meadow. Both night and day, they have sufficient grass to eat.

David's temple gates were effective for worship. They admitted the people to the presence of Jehovah, where they met with God and were renewed in their allegiance to him. But there was a temporary aspect to this. The worshipper would come back yet again for renewed rites of devotion. Jesus, as door, goes far beyond this. The sheep continually enjoy feeding through him. Perhaps the best-known sight of sheep is as they nibble at the grass. It is their way of life, as it were. Christ the door provides a constant source of lifelong, satisfying activity for the Christian. Mere religious observance can never provide this.

What a challenge to Christians! Is the gate of Scripture open or neglected, a vital source of instruction, warning, encouragement and training, or a closed book? Is the gate of prayer used or forgotten, a mere convenience in time of trouble, or an ongoing means of conversation with God? Is fellowship a figment of religious imagination, or a source of real stimulus as we bear one another's burdens and so fulfil Christ's law, or forgive one another's sins and discover the reality of Christ's love? Is growth in grace stunted, or spiritual development a regular feature of Christian experience? Christ, the effective door, challenges us to this. He turns our Valley of Achor into a door of hope: "'I tell you the truth, the man who does not enter the sheep pen by the gate but climbs in by some other way, is a thief and a robber...' Therefore Jesus said again, "I tell you the truth, I am the gate for the sheep. All who ever came before me were thieves and robbers, but the sheep did not listen to them. I am the gate; whoever enters through me will be saved. He will come in and go out, and find pasture. The thief comes only to steal and kill and destroy; I have come that they may have life, and have it to the full"' (John 10:1,7-10).

'Jesus answered, "I am the way and the truth and the life. No one comes to the Father except through me"' (John 14:6).

> People need the Lord, people need the Lord.
> At the end of broken dreams
> He's the open door.
> People need the Lord.

The cornerstone

David's prediction as he envisaged the temple building is fulfilled in Jesus, the *cornerstone* of the church. Here we find direct quotation rather than mere allusion. Indeed, Psalm 118 is the most frequently quoted of the Psalms throughout the New Testament. It is mentioned in all four Gospels, Acts, Hebrews and 1 Peter. The specific reference to the cornerstone is quoted in all the foregoing, except the Gospel of John and the letter to the Hebrews. The way in which the quotations occur is definite and precise. The meaning is both clear and instructive.

The prophet Haggai had encouraged King Zerubbabel that, although the second temple was inferior, so far as appearance was concerned, to the first temple, yet God would reveal his glory in that place. There God would give peace (Hag. 2:9). During the last six days of his life, standing in that very place, within the precincts of Herod's Temple, Jesus quotes words from Psalm 118:

'Jesus said to them, "Have you never read in the Scriptures:

""The stone the builders rejected
    has become the capstone;
the Lord has done this,
    and it is marvellous in our eyes'?

'"Therefore I tell you that the kingdom of God will be taken away from you and given to a people who will produce its fruit. He who falls on this stone will be broken to pieces, but he on whom it falls will be crushed."

'When the chief priests and the Pharisees heard Jesus' parables, they knew he was talking about them. They looked for a way to arrest him, but they were afraid of the crowd because the people held that he was a prophet'

                     (Matt. 21:42-46).

It was remarkable. Jesus identifies the religious leaders with the wicked tenants who kill the son of the owner of the vineyard in the parable. But to do this, Jesus quotes Psalm 118:22-23, implying that those who reject him as Messiah are crushed by the chosen corner-stone, while those who receive him come under its purposeful influence and are established. Christ the cornerstone either makes or mars, stabilizes or shatters, designs or destroys. Historically speaking, this meant that the gospel, after the Jews had rejected it, would be offered to Gentiles, a theme predicted in the Old Testament, affirmed by Jesus and fulfilled in the story of Acts. Practically speaking, it means that the gospel presents only two alternatives:

either reception of Christ as cornerstone leading to life, or rejection of him bringing death. This is because the Messiah, as cornerstone, while 'rejected by man' was 'chosen by God'. His kingdom would inevitably be established, regardless of man's response. The prophecy had reached a glorious fulfilment.

Peter writes of this in his first letter. Addressing persecuted believers scattered throughout Asia Minor, he assures them of their blessings in Christ the cornerstone (1 Peter 2:4-10). Design marks their entire experience of Christ. Christ has given them life. Coming to him, the living stone, they are built as living stones into God's temple. Christ has become precious to them. Because they believe in Jesus, he has become worthy in their eyes. He is no longer despised and rejected, but an object of their passionate devotion and warm love. Christ has related them, by means of covenant, to God. They are 'a chosen people, a royal priesthood, a holy nation, a people belonging to God' (1 Peter 2:9).

Peter also traces out the alternative. Destruction follows those who reject Christ the cornerstone. They stumble over Christ the rock. They disobey the gospel message. Their tragic destiny is inevitable. Again, there are the same two contrasting outcomes as in Jesus' teaching: making or marring, stability or shattering, design or destruction, purpose or confusion.

The source texts for this instruction include Psalm 118, linked with similar predictions from the prophet Isaiah. All the quotations recall the Messiah as cornerstone:

'As you come to him, the living Stone — rejected by men but chosen by God and precious to him — you also, like living stones, are being built into a spiritual house to be a holy priesthood, offering spiritual sacrifices acceptable to God through Jesus Christ. For in Scripture it says:

"See, I lay a stone in Zion,
     a chosen and precious cornerstone,
and the one who trusts in him
     will never be put to shame."

'Now to you who believe, this stone is precious. But to those who do not believe,

> '"The stone the builders rejected
>   has become the capstone,"

and

> '"A stone that causes men to stumble
>   and a rock that makes them fall."

'They stumble because they disobey the message — which is also what they were destined for.

'But you are a chosen people, a royal priesthood, a holy nation, a people belonging to God, that you may declare the praises of him who called you out of darkness into his wonderful light. Once you were not a people, but now you are the people of God; once you had not received mercy, but now you have received mercy'

> (1 Peter 2:4-10, quoting Isa. 28:16; Ps. 118:22;
>   Isa. 8:14).

People scattered throughout Asia Minor could be called 'a people belonging to God' through Christ the cornerstone. That was the ultimate proof that God had taken the kingdom from Jews and given it to Gentiles. It marks, too, the fulfilment of David's prediction about the stone, chosen by God and rejected by man: 'The Lord has done this, and it is marvellous in our eyes' (Ps. 118:23). The whole action was God's doing.

Too often people get the wrong idea about the gospel message. They spend a lifetime thinking that it is an offer which they can contemplate and, eventually, accept or reject. They even suppose that there is some middle course of neutrality, where they neither accept nor reject Christ but simply reserve judgement, a kind of 'safe agnosticism'. The gospel is not like that. Christ the cornerstone confronts man with inevitable authority. His is an overriding and incessant challenge in life. Christ is like Francis Thompson's 'Hound of Heaven', who pursues us 'down the nights and down the days, down the arches of the years, down the labyrinthine ways of my own mind'. Christ is also the Messiah of the psalmist's God.

> Behind, before me, thou dost stand,
> And lay on me thy mighty hand;

Such knowledge is for me too strange
'Tis high beyond my utmost range.

Oh, whither shall my footsteps fly
Beyond thy Spirit's searching eye?
To what retreat shall I repair
And find not still thy presence there?

(Metrical Psalm 139)

Christ pursues with 'strong feet, unhurrying chase, unperturbed pace'. At all stages of life, Christ confronts with his purpose, either in design or destruction: whether the young man, successful in examinations, looking forward to university, or new parents with a lovely home and a little baby, or those happily married over the years now taking delight in their grandchildren, or those experiencing sadness or difficulty — failure in business, financial anxieties, shattering grief. Whatever the joy or sorrow, Christ the cornerstone confronts and asks, 'Do you know my saving grace? Have you experienced my transforming purpose?' Without him, hopes are imperilled, intentions are soured and ultimate satisfaction lost. There are only the two alternatives: design or destruction. There is no middle course. The gospel of Christ the cornerstone offers no 'safe neutrality'. Those who are not for him are against him. Those who do not gather with him scatter abroad.

Christians must constantly rediscover the design of Christ as cornerstone in their lives. Too often this is lost or discarded in the rush of life. Sometimes a radical change is needed as God the Spirit breaks the mould of life to remake us.

Spirit of the living God, fall afresh on me
Break me, melt me, mould me, fill me;
Spirit of the living God, fall afresh on me.

Sometimes a yielding devotion to God, the skilful Potter, is necessary:

Lie still and let him mould thee,
O Lord, I would obey!
Be thou the skilful Potter
And I the yielding clay.

Bend me, oh, bend me to thy will
While in thy hand, I'm lying still.

(Ada R. Habershon)

Whatever the circumstances, Christ, the cornerstone, takes the weight of the building and shapes his design into all its parts: 'The Lord has done this, and it is marvellous in our eyes.'

Christ is made the sure foundation,
Christ the head and cornerstone,
Chosen of the Lord, and precious,
Binding all the church in one,
Holy Zion's help for ever
And her confidence alone.

(Latin 7th or 8th century;
translated by John Mason Neale)

The sacrifice

David's aspirations at the altar are fulfilled in Jesus, the final *sacrifice* for his people. As Jesus quotes Psalm 118:25-26, it gives rise to a significant sequence of events, which underline the climax of this processional psalm as fulfilled prophecy.

Jesus entered Jerusalem a week before his death. He borrowed a donkey and her colt for the purpose. Eventually, he used the colt. This was to fulfil the prophet Zechariah's prediction:

'Rejoice greatly, O Daughter of Zion!
    Shout, Daughter of Jerusalem!
See, your King comes to you,
    righteous and having salvation,
    gentle and riding on a donkey,
    on a colt, the foal of a donkey'

(Zech. 9:9).

The sign was not lost on the people of Jerusalem. Noting how the disciples spread their cloaks on the animals, a very large crowd laid their cloaks on the road. Their ancestors had done the same for Jehu, just prior to his proclamation as king (2 Kings 9:13). Others cut branches from the trees as garlands. But, above all, the crowds ahead started chanting 'Hosannas' or 'Save' calls from Psalm 118:

> "'Hosanna to the Son of David!"
> "'Blessed is he who comes in the name of the Lord!"
> "'Hosanna in the highest!"
>   'When Jesus entered Jerusalem, the whole city was stirred and asked, "Who is this?"
>   The crowds answered, "This is Jesus, the prophet from Nazareth in Galilee"'
>
> (Matt. 21:9-11; cf. Ps. 118:25-26).

The crowds were right. The true identity of Jesus, the prophet from Nazareth, was the Son of David. Jesus was the Messiah. This was clear both from his actions and words. The spectacle of a grown man on an undersized foal recalled Zechariah's prophecy and the people saw the significance of this. The disciples' behaviour confirmed their view. As an entire group, they acclaimed Jesus as Messiah. The whole scene was fraught with Messianic overtones. There was spontaneity as well. Children followed the example of the adults. The whole city was in such a stir that the teachers felt obliged to bring the matter to Jesus' attention (Matt. 21:15-16). Jesus entered Jerusalem acclaimed as Son of David at the head of the procession.

The sad thing about this fulfilment, as compared with the outcome in the psalm, was the people's change of heart. Within a week, the cries of 'Hosanna' had turned to 'Crucify', the waving palms to wagging heads, the acclamation of the Son of David to the call for the criminal Barabbas. The pregnant silence in the psalm had introduced the awesome spectacle of offered sacrifice. The clamorous voices of Jerusalem, once supporting Jesus, suddenly disclaimed their Messiah in the bitterest terms. Why ?

It was not just the sharpness of Jesus' actions and words during that last fateful week, or the judgemental strain of his teaching against the religious leaders. It was not even the subtle persuasiveness of the scribes and Pharisees, who suggested that sacrificing Jesus might embarrass, and even imperil, Roman authority. It was Jesus himself. He claimed to be Messiah, but in a very different way from what they had expected. There was one glaring difference between what they wanted and Jesus' view of his claims. He would be a suffering servant, not a triumphant king; the author of a kingdom of peace, in which his servants carried no arms, not a Jewish rebel ridding them of Rome's supremacy. A Messiah of a spiritual kingdom, who would die in self-sacrifice, was not what the people of Jerusalem wanted. They wanted a national leader, a defiant hero, not a deluded, religious idealist. So, instead of 'Hosanna!' they shouted 'Crucify!'. They declined Christ's offered sacrifice. They asked for Barabbas, not Jesus.

The story constantly repeats itself. Many, attracted with interest to Christ, are almost convinced to follow him. Then they change. They distance themselves from him, find fault with his teaching, grow sceptical of his claims and even begin to hate instead of love him. Why does this happen?

The underlying reason is precisely the same today as it was then: his demands are too absolute, his teaching too severe, his requirements too sweeping. The necessity of his death, as a sacrifice to cleanse from sin, is unacceptable. Does one really need that? The pattern of his death as an example to follow is impracticable. Can a Christian really go that far? People draw back from Christ the King and reject his claims. His sacrifice of cleansing and consecration are not for them. They know nothing even of David's shadowy aspirations regarding that sacrifice: 'The Lord is God and he has made his light to shine upon us' (Ps. 118:27), let alone of the full glory and brightness of God's love in Jesus the Saviour. Isaac Watts' view of Christ's death is completely lost on them:

When I survey the wondrous cross
On which the Prince of glory died,
My richest gain I count but loss,
And pour contempt on all my pride.

Forbid it, Lord, that I should boast,
Save in the death of Christ, my God;
All the vain things that charm me most,
I sacrifice them to his blood.

Were the whole realm of nature mine,
That were an offering far too small;
Love so amazing, so divine,
Demands my soul, my life, my all.

A personal view

Psalm 118 was Luther's favourite psalm. It 'had helped him out of troubles out of which neither emperor nor king, nor any other man on earth, could have helped him'. For all that Psalm 118 had previously meant to me, I found myself understanding, through my own experience as pastor, what Luther meant.

Raymond had contracted cancer of the throat. We did not suspect the gravity in those early days. Indeed, for some years there had been remission and we had almost forgotten the earlier illness. A young man, with a lovely wife and two daughters — how terrible the thought of anything terminal! But it did happen and it was terminal. I remember well those difficult days. Raymond and his wife were Christians and, amid all the turmoil, they looked to God for help. In a unique way, Psalm 118 became a source of comfort to Raymond, just as it had been to Martin Luther, especially verses 17-18:

'I will not die but live
  and will proclaim what the Lord has done.
The Lord has chastened me severely,
  but he has not given me over to death.'

We read that psalm over often together, reflecting on those particular words. The experience invested the psalm with fresh meaning for me. I began to think of the Messianic prophecies in the light of these earlier verses describing David's faith. Pictures of Jesus the door, the cornerstone, the sacrifice, became particularly precious.

Often I looked at Raymond in those anxious days. We had shared much together musically, socially, but, above all, spiritually. I remember his coming to faith and how he told me about it. The gospel word had got into his system, mastered his thoughts, convicted him of sin, hunted him down and led him to Christ the door. I watched him grow in grace as he attended church services and midweek meetings. I saw him fall in love with a Christian girl and marry. I saw God's covenant develop in his life, his two daughters both becoming Christians, the one using her gifts in song, the other her love of letter-writing in Christian service. Christ the cornerstone was moulding, shaping, developing the entire family. Then Christ's sacrifice came into view, not just in terms of cleansing but of consecration — total, absolute, final in Raymond's case. How often I asked the question, 'Why?' A young Christian man cut off in his prime, a heart-broken grieving widow, two girls losing a father they loved so much. But Raymond died in faith. I witnessed a growth in sanctification in his life in those closing days that I never thought possible. I saw him holding on to God's promise of life, amid severe chastening. When, eventually, the reality of death dawned, even then he did not doubt God's promise but took it with him to death itself. I pastored a grieving widow who, through loneliness, silence and tears, found the thread of faith and still loves her Lord. I saw Jesus' sacrifice on Calvary transforming the lives of his children, not only in terms of cleansing but of total consecration. Psalm 118 would never be the same to me again. Its meaning grows deeper and richer each time I think of those glorious words:

> I shall not die, but live, and shall
> Jehovah's works make known.
> The Lord hath me chastened sore,
> But not to death brought down.

> O set ye open unto me
> The gates of righteousness;
> Then will I enter into them
> And I the Lord will bless.

> This is the gate of God, by it
> The just shall enter in.
> Thee will I praise, for thou me heard'st,
> And hast my safety been.

> That stone is made head cornerstone,
> Which builders did despise:
> This is the doing of the Lord,
> And wondrous in our eyes.

> This day the Lord hath made, in it
> We'll joy triumphantly.
> Save, Lord, I pray thee: Lord, I pray
> Send thou prosperity.

Blest in the Lord's great name is he
That cometh us among;
We bless you from the house which doth
Unto the Lord belong.

God is the Lord, who unto us
Hath made light to arise:
Bind ye unto the altar's horns
With cords the sacrifice.

Thou art my God, I'll thee exalt;
My God, I will thee praise.
Praise ye the Lord, for he is good:
His mercy lasts always.

(Metrical Psalm 118).

The gate, the temple, the altar, so prominent in the procession of
Psalm 118, are all fulfilled in Jesus — the door, the cornerstone, the
sacrifice. Jesus is the new and living temple, who not only recreates
his people, as he calls them out of darkness into marvellous light, but
displays in their lives the virtues of his saving workmanship. Jesus
enlivens, shapes, houses and perfects the stones of this building, the
temple of the living God, built on himself the cornerstone. Jesus
personifies the temple of the Lord of Psalm 118.